Again!
Josh Jensen
April 7,

THE HEARTBREAK
GRAPE

Please
enjoy!
Josh Jensen

THE HEARTBREAK
GRAPE

A JOURNEY IN SEARCH OF THE PERFECT PINOT NOIR

Completely revised and updated edition

MARQ DE VILLIERS

McArthur & Company
Toronto

This paperback edition published originally in Canada in 2006 by
McArthur & Company
67 Mowat Avenue, Suite 241
Toronto, Ontario
M6K 3E3
www.mcarthur-co.com

Library and Archives Canada Cataloguing in Publication

**De Villiers, Marq, 1940-   The heartbreak grape : a journey in search of the
perfect pinot noir / Marq de Villiers.**

ISBN 1-55278-610-2

**1. Pinot noir (Wine)--California. 2. Wine and wine making--California.
3. Calera Wine Company. I. Title.**

TP557.D43 2006   641.2'223   C2006-903451-6

Design and composition by *Mad Dog Design Connection*
Printed in Canada by *Webcom*

The publisher would like to acknowledge the financial support of the Government of
Canada through the Book Publishing Industry Development Program (BPIDP) and the
Canada Council for the Arts, and the Ontario Arts Council for our publishing activities.
We also acknowledge the Government of Ontario through the Ontario Media
Development Corporation Ontario Book Initiative.

10 9 8 7 6 5 4 3 2 1

Grateful acknowledgement is made for permission to use undesignated excerpts from *Angels' Visits* by David Darlington published by Henry Holt and Co., copyright 1991.

Excerpt from *Proof*, by Dick Francis, is reprinted by permission of Sterling Lord Literistic Inc., copyright 1984 by Dick Francis.

CHAPTER ONE

*In which a bottle of wine is
consumed and some inquiries
into the grand conceit of its
origins are undertaken*

I n the palette of a warm California winter,
the early afternoon sky was a milky azure,
the sun just beginning to slant down over
the Gavilan Mountains across the valley, soft
in their rainy-season greenery. It's one of
those forever vistas, hills and deep gullies into the blue haze of
distance. The view takes in a wide white slash of eroded limestone hills, meadows spotted with gnarled live oaks, the muddy
blue of a pond down the sharp slope in front of us – that's the
San Andreas Fault down there, but I tried not to think of it, for
if it shook, as it very well might, we'd all go shuddering down
the slope, a prospect that needed no contemplation. On the
weathered picnic table on the terrace, pastrami sandwiches in
Styrofoam takeout containers, a plastic litre of no-name
mineral water, a bottle and three glasses of wine.

I picked up one of the glasses and stared through it at the mountains beyond. There was about an inch of wine left in the glass. I swirled it a little and stared again. The wine was a brilliant polished ruby, startling in its clarity. To the nose, the aromas were tantalizing, elusive; to the palate, the flavours a layered complexity of . . . I groped for the winetaster's vocabulary, but for the moment the words eluded me and in any case, it seemed to me, the colour was the key. The wine was a pinot noir from the Ryan Vineyard of the Calera Wine Company, and its maker, Josh Jensen, who was sitting across the picnic table with his back to the superlative view, had been making fine pinot noirs for . . . it occurred to me that he had been making these wines for almost 30 vintages now, and could no longer be called a radical innovator, a visionary, which were still the phrases used of him when I had last seen him, a decade or so earlier. Much had happened to Josh and his wines in the interim, much of it good though some of it anxiety-inducing, and much had happened in the same interim to the world of wines and especially the rarefied world of pinot noir, and not all of that was good at all. The intense, brilliant ruby of the Ryan pinot noir was in some way a clue to unlocking the complexity of those changes, as I would discover, coming as it did somewhere between the soda-pop pinky-fuschias of the cheaper offerings and the jammy beetroot purples of the expensive but blowsy pinots favoured by the critics of the moment. Like the world of wine itself, the world of pinot noir had been going through rapid changes. At first, there were hardly any California or New World pinot noirs of any consequence, and Josh Jensen's Calera was everybody's favourite exception – he proved that it could be done. Then suddenly there were pinot noirs all over the place, though not all of them good; then there was a movie about pinot noir, called *Sideways*, which was an unexpected hit, and all through this tastes were changing. Why they mutated is part of the story – the given reasons range from climate change to a craven toadying to influential critics – but mutate they did, and even venerable Burgundy, the home of some sublime (and some not so sublime) pinot noirs for two thousand years, was not immune, as we shall see.

It was more than 14 years earlier that I had first driven down from San Francisco to the picturesque little mission town of San Juan Bautista, then past Hollister to the Cienaga Road and so up into the Gavilan Mountains and the Calera winery.

On that day, outside on the same terrace, the sun was decanting over those same California hills, warm and still on an October afternoon, but inside the vaulted barrel-cellar the air was cool, damp, heady, vinous. Josh Jensen, who was then as now the owner, strategist and propagandist in chief of Calera (his business card simply calls him "Generalissimo" not out of hubris but in a sardonic disdain for titles of any kind), eased a plastic bung from one of the racked barrels, and it came away with a soft, sighing hiss, a faint carbonic prickle adding itself to the damp-oak and washed-earth and crushed-fruit smells of the winery. I closed my eyes and inhaled deeply and the aroma went directly, as aromas do, to the vaults in the brain where nostalgic memories are stored, and I remembered the great limewashed cellars of South Africa's Cape, where as a child I had played among oaken casks as big as houses, cool and serene despite the burning African sun. Memories welled up – farm workers in Wellington boots, unhurried and competent; lowing cattle, fresh hay, crushed grapes sticky with sugar, racks of bottles on dusty shelves, a cat sleeping in the entranceway, curled in the shade, a paw over its eyes. The farmer would bring visitors into the cellar, big buyers from the city, and they'd step over the cat and be seduced by the smells, and the farmer would draw off a little wine to taste, and after a while they'd leave, and the farmer would be smiling. In my memory he always seemed to be smiling.

I pulled my attention back to the cellar. Josh Jensen laid the bung on the barrel, alongside a small cloth and a plastic bucket. "These are made of some kind of acrylic compound. We don't use wood bungs any more. Who says we're against technology at our winery!"

Whoever it was, it hadn't been me. But this was a small phrase in a longer dialogue about winemaking, and I knew we'd come back to it. I did know that the old wooden bungs were always a problem for winemakers; after a while the moisture would wick up along the grain and the bung had to be wiped clean with sulphur dioxide or the wine would spoil. And if there was still fermentation going on in the barrel, the bungs could explode outwards; many a winemaker, incautiously leaning over the barrel, was banged on the head. Occasionally, someone lost an eye. The new soft acrylic stoppers were easy to get out and impervious to moisture.

There were four wineglasses on an upturned barrel that served as a table. Jensen picked up his "thief," a slender glass pipette about a foot long that looked rather like a turkey baster, and slipped it into the bunghole. He drew out enough wine to fill the glasses about a third. Sara Steiner, then Calera's assistant winemaker, and Diana Vita, the winery manager, picked up a glass each, and Josh picked up the third. The last was for me. I dipped my nose into the new wine. There was a strong fruitiness to the aroma, and underlying it a complex of other odours too elusive to detect, flowery, like crushed raspberries on a summer's day. I took a sip. It was tannic, and made my mouth pucker. Again, those elusive scents – there was an underlying silkiness that came from the oak, a faint hint of fresh farm butter.

I remember staring at the wine, as I did later, then into it, holding it up to the light. It glowed, that exact same brilliant polished ruby. I moved back a few paces, until the glass was framed in the doorway; beyond it I could see those high hills of the Gavilan range, folds after folds of gold, smooth and erotic, like the skin of an inner thigh. In the far distance the air was smoky, a blue haze melting into the golden grass. I could hear a cow mooing in the valley, a melancholy sound.

With difficulty, I turned away from the view. Josh Jensen was sniffing and swirling his glass. He peered at the label on the barrel. "Hmmm," he said. "Early picking from the Mills vineyard. New oak. Still very closed, but coming along nicely."

Steiner made notes. "Nice fruit," she said.

"Yes," Jensen said. "The late pickings will be less fruity than this, more opulent, much much more complex. Put them together and you'll have something wonderful here."

This last was directed at me, in an instructional and not propagandistic way – there's reason to believe that most of Josh Jensen's wines are wonderful in their way. I was there because I'd become interested in the obsessive quest for perfection in the making of high-end wines, and Jensen at his Calera winery was everywhere supposed to be making some of the best and most Burgundian pinot noir in America (a place where until recently you were not supposed to be able to make great wines from the pinot noir grape), and his notion of early, middle and late pickings in the vineyard was one small part of his technique – a part dropped for some years, now reincorporated. Although, when it came right down to it, I discovered later, I was really still missing the point. What he was telling me was, be respectful of the fruit – give it a bow as it passes through from vine to bottle, and don't get in its way more than you absolutely have to. I was somewhat reminded of a snatch of dialogue from a Dick Francis murder mystery called *Proof*, in which the hero is a wine merchant. The investigating cop, as stolid as most fictional cops, watched as the hero sold a bottle to a customer and dispensed advice along with it:

> *"You sell knowledge, don't you, as much as wine?"*
> *"Yeah. And pleasure. And human contact."*
> *"Is there anything you can't drink wine with?"*
> *"As far as I'm concerned . . . grapefruit."* He made a face. *"And that's from one,"* I said, *"who drinks wine with baked beans . . . who practically scrubs his teeth with it."*
> *"You really love it?"*
> I nodded. *"Nature's magical accident."*
> *"What?"*
> *"That the fungus on the grape turns the sugar in grape juice to alcohol. That the result is delicious."*
> *"For heaven's sake ..."*
> *"No one could have invented it,"* I said. *"It's just there. A gift to the planet."*

A gift of nature! Well, and so is the potato, I suppose. But no matter how crisp the *frite*, how silky the mash (no matter that the potato can be the colour of gold or a ghastly industrial blue), potato eaters and growers are not united into a community of interest in the way wine people are – potato shops are

not places where culture and agriculture meet (there's
only sound craft, to growing them); individual potato field
not change hands at astronomical prices; there are no specia
ized potato shops (1991 Yukon Golds, a great year!) or potato
tastings; no one collects vintage potatoes, or keeps cellar books
detailing their virtues. The potato is a humble thing and so, in
its way, is the vine.

I picked up my glass and carried it back to the doorway.
It now contained wine from a different barrel, and it too was
brilliantly clear, limpid. I took a sip, pulling it through my teeth
the way wine-tasters do. The vine, I thought, might be humble,
but wine is not humble at all. Wine has almost infinite variety
and complexity, able to give simple pleasure to millions of
people and at the same time to surprise and overwhelm the
most sophisticated palate. Wine is international, virtually
universal, with a history almost as old as man, with its own
litany and lore, with its own poetics of sensation, with its own
rituals (the formal tastings) and craft (more care is taken with
the barrels to store it in than with many complex industrial
artifacts). Winemaking can be an uncomplicated, automated
industrial process or a simple thing to do in a crock at home,
but the makers of great wine are magnificently obsessed, cease-
lessly self-questioning, constantly attempting to move their
product towards some elusive and ineffable ideal.

I looked out again at the California hills, and thought of
the community that wine represents. It stretches from Calera
across the Atlantic to the stony slopes of the Côte d'Or, in
Burgundy, still the centre of the pinot noir universe, and from
there to the drawing rooms of Knightsbridge, the salons of
Park Avenue, and the manor houses of the Hunter Valley.
Down the road from Calera, over the beautiful desolation of

ins, is the wine estate called Chalone,
...erior pinot noir and whose founder's life
...n's in interesting ways.

past the almond groves of the Central
...ve tank farms of the Gallo operation,
...come the closest of anyone to succeeding at that very
American task, the reduction of art to a diligent industrialism,
to chemistry, and marketing ... And yet the Gallos, marketers
par excellence (at the turn of the century, one out of every three
bottles sold in America was a Gallo wine), have also felt the
needle-pricks that tell them some things are beyond *process*,
and they are pouring money and resources into *quality*. I
thought when I first heard of their intentions that it would be
like trying to pour the Pacific Ocean through a funnel into a
five-gallon jug, like watching an ocean liner docking in a yacht
harbour. If they bring it off, I thought, their artistry will be
universally admired. If not, the purists would be confirmed in
their definitions of folly. And indeed, a decade later the third
Gallo generation had duly performed the miracle; one of their
wines from Sonoma even joined Calera and a score of others in
Paul Lukacs's 2005 book, *The Great Wines of America*. This was
not toadying, either. The wine made it on merit.

A little inland from Sacramento is the school of viticulture and enology of the University of California at Davis,
universally shortened to just "Davis," as in, "I don't want to be
a Davis-basher, but ..." These are the folks who brought you
that blue potato and the square tomato, for whom the chemistry of wine is their prime mandate. Davis has always been the
repository of enological orthodoxy, the proselytizer of viticultural hygiene, the Keeper of the Recipe, the people who made
possible the Gallos, the people who rescued the American wine

industry after Prohibition from oblivion (and also from the fruit fly, the vinegar bacterium, sundry diseases and pests), the people who have encouraged the production of good clean wines, well made, polished, safe, hygienic, characterless. How many times have I heard winemakers say of their new Davis recruits – people skilled at the chemistry of winemaking – that they first had to unlearn their Davis lessons before they could fully grasp, emotionally as well as technically, the idea of great wine. Or, at the least, they had to learn through mistakes to understand something profound about wine, which is that nature is older and far wiser than they are, and has more tricks up her provocative sleeve than can be discovered in the refractometers and centrifuges of the laboratory. They had to learn that what they did was not manufacturing, as they had been taught, but midwifery; they had to understand, as Colette wrote, that "wine makes the true savour of the earth intelligible to man." Nikos Kazantzakis, whose lush romanticism was once cherished in the fevered diaries of teenaged girls, called the drinking of wine "communion with the blood of the earth itself," a typically overwrought notion, but you get what he means.

Farther away, up the North Coast, and a million miles in sensibility from the jug wines that were the Gallos' early iteration, are the agricultural communities of Napa and Sonoma, where farmers have become successful through skill and superior marketing (there are people both humble and smug in both places; also people who've made for themselves an exceptionally gracious lifestyle – and hundreds and hundreds who merely went broke). Considerably north of Napa, in the Willamette valley of Oregon, are farmers toiling on the edge of climatic plausibility, as do the growers of the Côte d'Or in their venerable postage-stamp plots with their resonant names – the

Domaine de la Romanée-Conti, La Tâche, les Echézeaux, Clos de Vougeot.

The wine community stretches to the great merchants of New York and London, to the wholesalers, shippers, importers and distributors, to the fogs of Carneros in California, to the craggy peaks of the mountains around Fransch Hoek in South Africa, to the rare but fecund river valleys of Australia, to the fertile valleys of the central Chilean plains, to the stony fields of La Mancha and the gentle sheep meadows of New Zealand. And to the most surprising pastures – England, the Black Sea coast of Russia, even to that most unlikely of all *domaines*, Long Island. It reaches also from the *haute snob* wine shops of London through the idiosyncratic stores of New York to the massive warehouses of California (*Liquors and Ammo!* the signs will say) and down into the neighbourhood *boîtes* of Paris, where they sell the acidic plonk of *Algerie* and the Midi *en plastique*. And, finally, it reaches the millions of tables where the corks are pulled and the food is served and pleasure is given and taken.

There were only 12 barrels of the 1991 Early Mills vineyard pinot noir and 8 of the Late. The vineyard crews had only done two pickings that year; 1991, the tail end of a five-year drought, was a year of very small yields, even by Calera's famously parsimonious standards. We moved on down the rows of neatly stacked barrels, Josh Jensen using the thief at each one to draw out enough to fill our four glasses. We swirled, sipped, spat into the concrete runnels along the floor, Jensen carefully pouring the unused and untasted wine back into the barrels to top them up. Each barrel had a paper docket label stapled to the oak, and a stencil denoting its originating cooperage and its year. The dockets would contain scribbles, in various hands and in various coloured inks, some of them cryptic to the point of inscrutability – what did "CWPN87J 13" mean? (Calera winery pinot noir 1987 Jensen vineyard 13 barrels, if you must know.) Other notations were more straightforward:

10/15/91

MILLS EARLY

1/11 finished m-1

1/22 90 ppm So2

2/7 30 ppm So2

which simply meant the wine had been put into barrel on October 15, had finished its secondary, or malolactic, fermentation by November 1, and was twice stabilized by small doses of the anti-oxidant sodium dioxide, first on January 22 and then again on February 7.

The barrel also bore the notation that it had been made in France by the *tonnellerie* – cooperage – called François Frères, of St. Romain on the Côte d'Or in France, and a large "1-4" – it had been made in April 1991.

I would discover more on all these matters later.

Clear differences emerged as we moved along the rows. The Mills Early was a touch more astringent, the Mills Late much softer. Steiner was making notes on a small clipboard. She'd write down her own observations, and some of the comments of the others. "Green tannin," "very consistent," "rich oaky," "a little flat," "quite closed." Is the Early a little lean, the Late a little "top-heavy"? That's good – each picking contributes its character to the amalgam of the finished wine.

The oak taste of the wine from new barrels, about a third of the batch, was clearly evident – it contributed much of the silky, buttery quality. Josh said he could tell the difference between the barrels of François Frères and his other suppliers, whose barrels, he said, made the wine taste a hint too "resiny."

I asked him why that was so.

"I don't know," he said, somewhat disarmingly. "It's just that pinot noir and François Frères are friends. Or at least, my wines and François Frères are friends."

These samplings will continue every couple of weeks throughout the 15 months the wine is in barrel. Comparisons are made, progress noted. If something is going wrong in a barrel – as it occasionally does – they'll know it soon enough, and either correct it, if it's correctable, or eliminate it from the batches marked for later amalgamation. Afterwards, it will either be sold at a few pennies a gallon to a distillery, or will be poured away, the precious juice soaking into the parched California earth.

That morning, one of the barrels was marked to be kept separate from the others, to be kept away from the composite finished wines. The vines from which the juice came were grown with a new experimental trellis system, and Jensen wanted to know if he could detect a difference in the finished wine. This would happen in other years too; experimentation in the vineyards is ceaseless. In the early 2000s, new vineyards were planted, almost all of them in pinot noir, and all much more densely packed per acre than had been the norm at Calera hitherto; along with this were constant trials of new trellising systems, and in 2006 the vineyard manager abandoned the modified cordon system of pruning for a less neat but (he believed) more efficient pruning arrangement.

After our tasting, Steiner would do sample composites from the various Mills vineyard batches, and run analyses in her lab. I asked her what she was looking for.

"Just making sure everything is right," she said, "but it's also for me. I've only been here a short time, since August. This is my first Calera vintage. I want to use these tests to get to know the personalities of the different vineyard parcels, and the characters of the wines they make."

Steiner has gone now – she only made a few vintages – and was followed in short order by Belinda Gould, Terry Culton and now Corneliu Dane. Dane, a Romanian by birth with a strong technical training in food chemistry, nevertheless uses much the same vocabulary as the others. He talks about letting the vines teach you about the wines they will make. After four vintages, he said, he felt he was beginning to understand the personalities of the various vineyard parcels.

Personalities? Characters? And the other words so casually used around serious winemakers – Forwardness? Reserve? Shyness? Approachability? Seductiveness? Eagerness? Listening to winemakers can sound more like a debutantes' ball than a serious business, the kind of anthropomorphizing that would turn the stomachs of the professors at Davis, where they prefer to believe that flavour can be captured through rigorous analysis of long-chain polymers and that winemaking is essentially applied chemistry. But then in Jensen's view, theirs is a barren exercise. He believes they haven't learned the first thing about the craft – that to make good wine is a skill but to make great wine is an art; that wine can be cherished into excellence as well as manufactured; that winemaking is an emotional as well as an industrial task; that the search for perfectibility is a legitimate and a grand obsession. He thinks the professors are boring. They think he takes unnecessary risks for invisible returns.

It's one of the great things about wine, though. Everyone is right.

I was in the Calera cellars because of a particular bottle of wine.

After a while I'd come to think of it, somewhat portentously, as The Bottle, though there was nothing portentous about the place its cork was pulled, a comfortable suburban dining room in the comfortable middle-class enclave of Mount Vernon, New York, and certainly nothing pretentious about the host who pulled its cork or the guests who drank the proffered wine.

It was December and there was a log fire crackling in the hearth. The room was painted in honey yellow; there were piles of books everywhere (the host had been a publisher) and there was a striking ink drawing of the hostess on the wall, her beautiful Renaissance profile in graceful outline. The host took the bottle from his "cellar," a small cupboard underneath the stereo, and pulled the cork without comment, pouring a little of the wine into glasses on the table. I remember that something struck me about its clarity, a brilliant red, like rubies under fire, and though my memory is probably coloured by the warmth of the setting, I know I felt there was something . . . unusual . . . about it.

I looked at the label. It was simple, typographically elegant in an old-fashioned way, with very few words. Not as prolix as many California wine labels, no original artworks, no drawings of swooping eagles, hawks, prancing stags or the other wildlife so beloved of logo designers. There was a stylized drawing at the top of the label, in a small panel; it looked rather like the entrance to a fort of some kind. Underneath, in black Caslon typeface, were the words, Calera Jensen Mt. Harlan Pinot Noir, and underneath the vintage year, 1987, in the same burgundy colour as the drawing. Underneath that it said, in much smaller letters, "Grown, produced and bottled by Calera

Wine Company, Hollister, California." And still smaller, in italic script, *Table Wine.*

So Calera was the producer. What did "Jensen" mean? Why was it in the largest type on the label? And where was Mt. Harlan?

I turned the bottle around to read the explanatory label on the back. This was more helpful. It consisted of a map of the Calera vineyards, shown as small crosshatched patches on a white background, of varying size and orientation, four drawn in the same burgundy colour as the front label and two in green. A wiggly black line labelled Indian Creek ran through the north part of the label, a line which I much later discovered had been and still was a source of bitterness and heartbreak at the winery. A small arrow pointing west said "Pacific Ocean 23 mi," and another arrow denoted north. Each crosshatched patch was identified: Selleck vineyard, 5 acres (north of Indian Creek); Reed vineyard, 5 acres; Jensen vineyard, 14 acres; Mills vineyard, 12 acres. And the two green patches: chardonnay vineyard, 6 acres; viognier vineyard, 2 acres.

Underneath all this was a small paragraph: "These vineyards are planted on rare, limestone soil in the Gavilan Mountains of San Benito County. They are located 90 miles south of San Francisco, at 2,200 feet elevation. The Selleck, Reed and Jensen were planted in 1975. The Mills, chardonnay and viognier were planted in 1984."

The Mt. Harlan of the front label was not shown, though it presumably was one of the Gavilan Mountains of San Benito County. Chardonnay was familiar enough, and viognier I knew as an aromatic varietal native to the Rhône, and until recently seldom seen in North America, but what (or who) were Selleck, Reed, Jensen and Mills?

I took a sip, but my attention was drawn away from the wine by the person to my left, who was expounding on the legacy of Boris Yeltsin, and another conversation to my right, as the host described the arrival of a first grandchild. It wasn't until much later, after a second slice of beef *en croute* had disappeared, and the host poured the last of the Calera Jensen, that I turned back to the wine. This time I paid more attention, dipping my nose into the glass and inhaling slowly, then taking a small sip. It was rich and complex, with a maddening hint of chocolate and violets. I groped for descriptives, as wine people do, without much luck.

"Very nice, isn't it?" said the man to my left, before moving on from Yeltsin to the problems of advertising in a society of high demand and scarce goods. He meant the wine, not the Russian economy.

Nice, yes. It was certainly that.

I wanted to ask the host how much it cost, and where he got it, and where it came from, and how he'd discovered it, but there's nothing more boring at a dinner party than a quiz master, and I resisted. Still, I resolved to find out answers to these questions and more. How had the bottle got here? What made the host choose it? What forces of marketing, advertising, retailing put it in his hands? What distribution chain made it possible? What pricing strategy? Did the winemaker make any money from it, or did the middlemen take more than their share? Had the wine writers, those arbiters of vinous fashion, had their say? Had the wine won tastings? The wine was superb – how was it made, in some high-tech factory operation, by some imported Burgundian *maître de chai*, or by some inspired amateur, a refugee from the dental schools of California? How was the finished wine shaped by the vinification methods chosen? Who was the winemaker and what did he think of his art? What was the winery like? What was Mt. Harlan like? What did the label mean, rare limestone soil? What did that have to do with anything? How long had the winemaker been making wine – the label said the Jensen vineyard had been planted in 1975 – how long does a vine need to mature to produce grapes which make wine like this? What is the climate like at the vineyards and how did it affect the wine? Why pinot noir in the first place? I knew that farmers in California had long referred to it as the "heartbreak grape" because of its fickle nature and its tendency to veer wildly from thin plonk to superb *vins de garde*. Why did this winemaker, whoever he was, have the presumption to believe he could make wine of this quality? Where did he get the vines in the first place? Who planted them? Who cared for them and how? How were they watered, up there in the mountains?

And, most fundamentally, at what point did this winemaker first conceive of making this wine? Could I identify that moment, and trace the wine through its long journey from that moment of conception to this moment here, the wine being poured into a glass at a small dinner party in Mt. Vernon, New York?

The rest of the meal passed without further comment on the wine. The guests were not wine snobs, and they were content with good food and something good to drink.

It struck me that the winemaker would, in all probability, be content with that as well. If it was true that making fine wine is an art, the purpose of that art is to bring pleasure, and the unknown (to me) maker of Calera Jensen had certainly achieved that.

CHAPTER TWO

*In which a (formerly) ugly winery is found in
a beautiful if unstable place and
the people are encountered who sent
our bottle into the world*

Before venturing to San Francisco – I was living in Toronto then – I spent some time reading about Jensen and Calera in the wine press. I found that Josh (Jonathan) Jensen was much admired there, even venerated, and I was immediately satisfied that a journey in search of this perfect pinot noir would not be time wasted. His wines were judged "sublime" by Robert Parker, the über-critic, whose prose can be as purple as the cheap wines of the Midi but whose trenchant judgments can make or break a wine, a vintage or a winery. (We will have more to say about Parker in due course.) I had seen Jensen's picture in the *Wine Spectator*, hobnobbing with visiting Burgundian eminences, though the *Spectator's* prose about the man and his wines seemed to me a little more grudging. (There'll be more about the *Spectator*, too.) I had read about his winery in Oz Clarke's splendid book, *The New Classic Wines*. I had read reviews of his wines in *Vanity Fair* and *New York* magazine and the London *Sunday Telegraph*, among others. I had even read about him in the pages of *Toronto Life*, in the words of James Chatto. The only thing all these writers agreed on was that he made Burgundy-style wines, red and white, approaching and sometimes surpassing the great wines of Burgundy itself.

I called him from Toronto. "I want to do a book about a bottle of your wine," I said.

"Sure you do," he said. He sounded cordial, but his scepticism was easily apparent. I could almost hear the sub-text: *how many free bottles does this one want?*

"No, really," I insisted.

He wasn't really convinced. We went back and forth a bit and finally I said, "Why don't we meet in San Francisco and we can talk it over?"

We agreed to meet for breakfast at the hotel I preferred, the Griffon, on the waterfront near the Embarcadero. He never made it but promised to make a reservation in the hotel's dining room, the Roti, a current favourite of the city's foodies, and said he'd meet me there. He forgot the reservation, but showed up 20 minutes later looking somewhat frazzled, and we settled down over a bottle of "not bad" chardonnay (not his own). He was in town for a weekend visit with his three kids, who then lived in the city with his ex-wife, Jeanne.

Buried in all the prose about his wines and his winery were a few words about the man himself. Oz Clarke had called him "laid back and fired up at the same time, and slightly careworn." *Wine* magazine called him "weather-beaten." The *Houston Post* called him "feisty and confident ... a complicated man." The Swiss publication *Divo* called him the "intellectual outsider of the wine business." Across the table, I could see what they all meant. He has a long Scandinavian face, somewhat mournful in repose. It reminded me of a horse, though I mean this well: the horse is the most elegant of creatures, with its long bones and expressive lips and slyly intelligent eyes. Jensen's is the face of a man who is outdoors much of the time; and since he was then almost 50, the squint-lines were settling in for good. The body was long and rangy, like one of those Nordic skiers you always see crossing the 50-kilometre finish line at the Olympics minutes ahead of anyone else. Big hands, big bones, big opinions – on American politics (he's a libertarian), on the "eco-terrorists" of California, on his own and other wines, on almost anything he has an articulated, clearly thought out position. After the chardonnay we ordered a bottle of his own Mills single-vineyard pinot noir – he always eats in restaurants that serve his own wines except when he indulges his passion for sushi, when he usually takes a bottle of his own along. I watched as he began to systematically demolish a spit-roasted chicken, done rare. In a while the chef came out to ingratiate himself. After a little mutual stroking ("I've always admired your wines ..." "There were so many good things on the menu I had trouble making up my mind ..."), the chef retired to his stoves and Jensen gave a wry smile. "I'm as much a marketer as a winemaker these days," he said. "Very much part of the business."

Finally persuaded I was serious and not just trying to score some wine on the cheap, he agreed that we'd meet at the winery the next morning. I was greatly looking forward to it. Almost everyone who'd written about the Calera wine operation described it as being located in the "remote Gavilan Mountains," as if they had somehow found themselves in exurban Ulan Bator. For example, the *Companion Wine Review*, in its Spring 1991 issue, referred to "Josh Jensen's bandit hideaway in the Gavilan Mountains, kind of near Chalone Vineyards if you happen to have a Bell Ranger." In truth, Calera is not that remote in geographical terms, being less than an hour inland from Monterey and Carmel and not very far from the main Los Angeles San Francisco freeway. But in sensibility and feeling it is remote – and remote indeed from the verdant hillsides of Napa or Sonoma, a hundred and fifty miles to the north.

Much has changed since that first visit, but then the winery was not a place that clasped visitors to its bosom. There was no entrance sign to speak of, just a breakneck turn to the right off Cienaga Road and a scratched and battered galvanized mailbox, much shot-up by passing hunters, with the name Calera barely visible. A few yards up the gravel road there was a sign that declared winery tours to be by appointment only, and farther in another sign, in pure Jensenese, that said

> *Stop! Go Back!*
> *Landmines and rattlesnakes ahead!*
> *Authorized personalities only beyond this point!*
> *Calera Wine Company.*

The road to Jensen's house bears left – it's also the road to the maintenance sheds, and where the trucks carrying the grapes will go when they deliver them to the hoppers. To the right, down a sharp incline, is the road to the winery office.

The vineyards are several miles away in reality and a

million miles away in feeling. If the winery is remote, the vineyards might as well be the deep Sahara. Turn right off the Cienaga Road onto Limekiln Road, and a mile or two in there's a rambling brown house that belongs to Calera's vineyard manager, Jim Ryan. From there, a small dirt road goes up a steep slope. The road winds sharply up the mountain. There are no guard rails and a precipitous, nerve-wracking drop to the right. Near the top is a relatively flat plateau, and a locked gate. Past a few cattle pastures, another gate. Beyond that is the Calera reservoir, the subject of almost as many stories as the winery (for years Jensen fought a war of attrition against the ecology bureaucrats, a secretive mining company he suspected of wanting his hilltop, and sundry other parties), and the first of his vineyards, six acres of chardonnay.

There are no power lines to the mountaintop. Fuel for the diesel pumps must be trucked up that appalling road.

The soil on the roads and in the vineyards is reddish white, almost chalky in texture. There are deer everywhere, unsurprised and audacious. In the woods are wild boar. There are rattlesnakes, skunks and gophers, rabbits and birds, and tarantulas on the roads. I stepped gingerly past one, which paused to look me over before scuttling – arrogantly, I thought – into the bushes. This is not the perfect place for a gentle *dejeuner sur l'herbe*. The limestone kiln pictured on Calera's labels ("Calera" is Spanish for limekiln) is still there, way up in the mountains, and even higher, much higher than the vineyards, are the ruins of a rock-crushing plant.

On the right are 15 rows of chardonnay. Further up the canyon are the viognier plantings, on 6.1 acres. Up beyond these are two shallow wells, a few storage tanks for water and two more reservoirs, empty and with great runnels punched through them by a bulldozer, and more vineyards. During my first visit a crew was brushing land where the 13.1-acre Ryan vineyard was eventually planted in 1998 and 2001. To the right of the access road are the other named pinot noir plantings, the 14.4-acre Mills, the 13.8-acre Jensen, the 4.4-acre Reed and the 4.8-acre Selleck, all of them on steep slopes at crazy angles to the road, facing every which way – the various Mt. Harlan vineyards swing almost completely around the cone-shaped mountaintop. Between the Jensen and the Mills is a large block of 15.6 acres, still unnamed in 2006, and merely called Yellow, Red and Green zones. The vines there are all pinot noir, but Jensen is not happy with the wines they produce and has yet to take any to market. The Mills, chardonnay and viognier vineyards were planted in 1984. The Selleck, Reed and Jensen were planted in 1975, except for 500 plants in the Jensen, which were set a year earlier as an experiment. Where the plants came from is something of an underground legend in California pinot noir circles.

The wineries of South Africa where I grew up were always – *always* – beautiful as well as functional, and I came to think of beauty as part of the trade, as an integral part of the business. How could it be otherwise? These wineries were always set in the rock-ribbed blue mountains of the Cape, in the green and verdant folds in those mountains, and the buildings in which they were housed were the gracious manors in the style called Cape Dutch – low, elegant, thatch-roofed, their limewashed walls thick and cool. Even the cellar buildings at Groot Constantia outside Cape Town were grand enough to pass as a gracious château elsewhere; the Great House at Boschendal in the Drakenstein Mountains, where my family began its South

African sojourn, is now a national monument, and beautiful beyond compare. The wineries I had visited in France were always at least grand, if occasionally ugly and assertive in that peculiarly French bourgeois manner. Even in America there are treasures: I had recently spent an idyllic couple of hours in Sonoma at the Iron Horse Winery, whose hundred-year-old house, meticulously kept and lovingly filled with antiques and objets d'art, is nestled in a stand of ancient sycamores and cedars.

But Calera was not originally built as a manor house, or a gentleman's residence, or as a refuge from the city for a wealthy lawyer. It was built as a rock-crushing plant, part of a failed attempt to grind up Mt. Harlan into cement, gravel and granite blocks. Everyone who wrote about it agreed that it was functional, efficient and – not to put too fine a point on it – ugly.

True assessments all. Though "ugly" is no longer just.

Even before the recent upgrades, for which see later in this chapter, the plant had other virtues. As Oz Clarke put it, "The buildings may be ugly – what rock-crushing plant isn't? – but Calera's owner saw behind the daunting tangle of old weather-stained concrete and rampant weeds something all quality winemakers would love to possess – an entirely gravity-fed winery. At the top of the eight levels (actually, there are seven) he could bring in his boxes of grapes. At the bottom level he could store his bottles to sell. In between, each movement of grape or wine could be by the gentlest of forces – that of gravity."

For Jensen the advantage of a gravity flow winery is that it eliminates mechanical pumping and handling, and his obsession (or one of his many obsessions) is with minimal handling of the wine during production.

Of course here, in this particular part of California, gravity has another and possibly more sinister meaning. In Hollister, the nearest town, residents had long ago become used to watching parts of their houses drifting slowly away, or tilting, or, indeed, seeing their neighbours' houses slowly getting closer. The Cienaga Road is plumb in the middle of what the U.S. Geological Survey calls the Creeping Zone of the San Andreas Fault – viz. that pond, easily visible from Calera's terrace. Indeed, the Cienaga Road *is* the San Andreas Fault, which in geological terms is nothing more than a shifting subterranean rubble pile ground between two massive continental plates. Should the Really Big One ever occur, the Calera winery, which is on the very lip of the Pacific Plate, will slide past its neighbours on the other side of Cienaga Road, who are firmly anchored to the North American Plate, and disappear into the newly created abyss.

I asked Jensen if the thought ever bothered him, but he gave me that puzzled shrug that all Californians affect when asked the question.

The winery consists of seven levels of retaining concrete walls cascading vertically down the hillside. When the rock-crushing plant was converted to a winery, the engineers insisted on setting reinforcing concrete grade beams in a continuous band from top to bottom, at each level penetrating the earth to 30 or 35 feet, and at the same time slung steel I-beams between the verticals. Still, in the '89 earthquake, a three-ton wine press "twirled like a spinning top" on the upper level of the winery. "However, we didn't lose a drop, not a bottle or a cask." In fact, Calera helped press grapes for another winery, that of David Bruce, which was badly damaged in the quake.

Jensen described his unusual operation in a Spring 1990

mailer to his regular customers, because, as he wrote (laying the irony on pretty thick):

"Hardly anyone actually visits the winery. Already this year we've had two visitors, and it's only March. We may get two or three more before next winter's snow arrives and cuts us off from the outside world once again. Of course, the two visitors who did find us ran quite a few risks getting here: flat tires courtesy of the puncture weeds, attacks by killer bees, and then there are always those pesky rattlesnakes and crazed wild boar – they make better sausages than neighbours."

The top level is a roadway leading to the maintenance sheds several hundred yards further up the hillside. Part of it is paved to make it easier for the trucks from the vineyards. The grapes arrive in half-ton food-grade plastic bins on a flatbed trailer, and forklifts dump them into hoppers. They fall into one of the seven stainless steel fermentation tanks a level below. These are massive things, eight or ten feet tall and wide enough to comfortably contain your average five-piece bathroom. They're all round but two, the largest, which fit exactly between the concrete grade beams. Below these tanks are Calera's presses, covered with bright blue tarps when they're not in use.

These are state of the art, exceptionally expensive German stainless steel presses of 15,000-litre and 4,500-litre capacity. "For a small operation we have very fancy presses," Jensen acknowledges. From the presses the wine is drawn down another level through flexible food-grade plastic hoses into two large stainless steel tanks, 4,500-gallon and 6,000-gallon capacity. These have been sprayed on the outside with a white insulation coating, and are used only for short-term storage and "settling." From there the wine drops another level to the cellars, where it's stored in barrel. After 15 months in barrel it's drawn off, again by gravity feed, into fining tanks and thence to the bottling plant on the warehouse level.

For many years the three upper levels, the fermenting tanks, presses and holding tanks, remained unroofed, exposed to the elements, tarps their only protection. A roof was always planned "as soon as we can afford the $100,000 it would cost." Only the lowest four levels were covered, with a 13,000-square-foot galvanized metal roof. The widest portion is the lowest, the warehouse level. Thence, as Jensen put it in his mailer, "we ship our rare and precious products to a thirsty world."

A small corner of all this, squeezed between two of the grade beams, was marked out in the proprietor's head for an office. For more than 20 years the "office" was a construction trailer on blocks in front of the winery itself. Inside the trailer were two rooms and a large closet. One room was the winemaker's "lab" – here in quotes because it was so laughable. The other room was for the office help and winery management, as well as a dusty photocopy machine, several newish computers, and a coffee maker. The winery staff acknowledged a little ruefully that "it would be nice" to have better quarters.

Another corner of the plant was earmarked for a tasting and hospitality room, but this was low on everyone's list. It would have to wait until Calera's multiple water problems were solved, until a new bottling line was set in place, and the two upper levels roofed. If visiting chefs came to Calera (which they occasionally did), bringing a feast with them, they were obliged to set up trestle tables in the warehouse, just as the staff did in 1991 for a high-powered French delegation from Burgundy, come to see what all the fuss was about.

It was always clear that Jensen would spend on his beloved wines sooner than he'd spend on himself or his staff. The staff knew this and were wryly affectionate about it – they, too, were loyal to the wines.

Still, that all changed in 2001. Jensen's single-vineyard pinot noirs were white-hot in the marketplace (they were even being rationed to customers), and so were his chardonnays. The worst drought years were, at least temporarily, over, and the new vineyards planted and producing. So he paid another visit to his "dear bank," as he wryly calls it, and came away with a cheque for somewhere around two million dollars for new vineyards and for the winery extensions and additions.

It was absolutely the worst time to borrow money in the wine business (tourism and with it the restaurant business collapsed, the dot-com bust, the stock market meltdown, 9/11, the worldwide wine glut and the rest), but it must be said that the money was intelligently spent.

The first to go up was the roof over the upper levels, a rakish, angular thing that did, indeed, cost $100,000 to construct. Then the trailer was consigned to the dump and a massive new two-story edifice attached to the front of the old winery. Suddenly Calera was not ugly at all, but stylish in a high-industrial motif, all stainless steel and glass with polished wood floors. A sophisticated new lab was added (no more keeping bacterial cultures with the staff's coffee cream) and new computers all round. On the second floor, a panoramic sweep of windows gave out to that same magnificent view; Jensen himself occupied the corner space, with a ramp leading off to his house, and the staff were spread along the curtain of glass. At one end was a glass dining table for lunches, and in the centre, near the staircase, was a moose head from Canada and a couple of African ungulates, there for no apparent reason but whimsy. Along the southwest façade an array of solar panels helped heat water to elevate the temperatures in those parts of the barrel vaults where secondary fermentations were being encouraged. The "tasting room" remained a couple of planks on upturned barrels, but winery tours were now encouraged (though still by appointment) and there was even a sign on the highway.

Some of the two million was spent on vineyards. Nineteen new acres were laid out.

Calera lost money in 2002, 2003 and 2004. The staff retrenched (all, including the proprietor, taking a pay cut), but no one was fired and in 2005 the winery had its best dollar-year ever, with sales and dollar volume up 40 per cent. "Wine is a cyclical business, but that trough was lower than any," Jensen says now.

At the end of my first visit, in 1992, I poked about for an hour or two, dodging tarantulas and brooding about the San Andreas Fault a few hundred yards downhill, and then, before I left for the day, marshalled the winery staff outdoors for a photograph.

At the beginning of 2006, I took another staff photo. They shuffled out, looking sheepish, and stood in a stiff line for the camera. There were a number of them in both photos. Generalissimo Jensen, of course, winery manager Diana Vita and her assistant Judy Ferreira (now Judy Vargas), cellar master Abraham Corona and his brother Adolfo were all veterans. Some were new – there was a third Corona brother, Pedro, and an addition to the office staff, Dora Del Real. And of course winemaker Sara Steiner was gone, replaced (after several interim appointments) by Corneliu Dane, now in his fourth harvest. Utility worker Dave Larsen, whom I remembered from before, had retired; he was to be replaced the day after my visit by Daniel Banderas. Missing were national sales manager Marta Rich, who works from her home in Sonoma County, a young Danish apprentice, Margit Svenningsen, who works part-time in the lab, and the two women, also part-timers, who ran the weekend tasting operations, Lori Pinatelli and Kathleen Smith.

There were just eight in the 2006 picture. I've looked often at this photograph, and the one from 1992, staring at the lineup, trying to see anything that would say, here are the people who produce one of the world's great wines. But it's no use. No one could possibly guess from the picture what these people do for a living. They're dressed in all-Americana: jeans, T-shirts, sweaters, sneakers, one or two pairs of boots, an overall. There's nothing glamorous about them, nothing particularly dull. If there are a few more Hispanic faces than would be the American norm, well, this is California. They could be a suburban bowling club, a law office out for a picnic, a busload of Presbyterian missionaries, anything.

I asked Jensen for an annotated reading on his staff, just as I had a decade earlier.

Corneliu Dane was the assistant winemaker. Steiner had been followed as winemaker by Belinda Gould and Terry Culton, neither of whom lasted more than three years (and both of whom, Jensen said in an unguarded moment, "thought they were geniuses after one vintage and wanted to change everything"). Though paid as winemaker, Dane was explicitly hired as assistant winemaker, because who has the final say in winemaking decisions is often a tricky point of protocol in wineries.

In many small operations, especially those owned by wealthy urban refugees, dentists, lawyers, or filmmakers like Francis Ford Coppola, the hired winemaker is the final arbiter of taste, the governor of the house style, the person who controls the decision-making process. In other wineries, whether massive operations like Gallo, or boutiques like Calera, where the obsession of the owner is what drives the whole operation, the winemaker mostly serves as the quality-control expert, the person who uses chemistry to approximate the owner's art, the person who gives rhythm and timing to the owner's instinct.

Jensen had already told me that Dane had a strong technical background. He graduated from the University of Bucharest in Romania with a master's degree in food science; after that he worked for a few years in a brewery, and then ran his own restaurant. Six years ago he and his wife – also a winemaker – came to the United States. Corneliu was simply looking for work, any work, in the food business, but he arrived in California in September, at harvest time, and within days was hired at Kendall Jackson as a temporary worker. In a year he was promoted to research enologist, and two years after that to production enologist. It was then he spotted Jensen's ad for an assistant winemaker, and came calling. "Calera is a little different," he said with some understatement. Kendall Jackson had some two million gallons of wine in stainless steel tanks, and somewhere around 45,000 oak barrels; when Dane left, the winery was in a major expansion of its barrel program. Calera, by contrast, has fewer than 1,000 barrels, and produces a mere 30,000 cases from vineyards that eke out the lowest yields-per-acre of any in the business. The assistant winemaker thing didn't bother him at all. He wanted to learn to make the best wines he could. He even agreed not to suggest any changes at all for the first year, while he came to understand the operation, an undertaking he managed to keep, Jensen says, "mostly."

Calera's most senior executive, winery manager Diana Vita, trained as an enologist and lab tech. She moved to the Central Coast area from Napa, where she had worked for several larger wineries as a chemical technician. She and her husband landed in a vintage log house in Big Sur, and set up a small winemaking operation of their own. In 1992 she was also raising kids and commuting an hour to get to work in Calera every day, and it was a matter of some debate how long she would want to continue leading three or four lives, but in 2006 she showed no sign of going anywhere. "She just showed up one day and asked if we needed someone to crank out assays," Jensen says. "She was just going to be a two-day-a-week lab person, but now she runs the business. Ever since she's arrived she's been part of our tasting panel. She's been here for almost 20 years or so now, and she has a longer historical take on what we do and what our wines are like than anyone except me.

"The three cellarmen, the Corona brothers, are all Mexicans. They work the barrels, pressing and crushing, bottling and so on, they're great, they're the real reason for our success. They're hard working, smart, confident, a reliable bunch of guys." Daniel Banderas will help them out.

What about the vineyard crew, who weren't at the winery for my picture-taking?

"The manager is Jim Ryan, who has been with us since 1979. He took a college course in viticulture, grape farming, at CalPoly, now called California State University Polytechnic at San Luis Obispo, one of the major farm colleges in the state, along with UC Davis and Fresno State."

Like most farmers, Ryan mistrusts change, but since Jensen began prodding him some years ago to convert the operation to more "organic techniques" he has become a convert, and most days can be seen up at the estate's massive compost heap, peering under its black canvas covers to inspect this other kind of fermentation. "Bird shit, cattle dung and grape pomace, mostly," he told me proudly, and the formerly brittle soil in the vineyards now has earthworms and micro-organisms down to 30 feet. With the expanded vineyard acreage, Ryan manages a crew of seven full-time workers, including equipment manager Shawn Callaghan. Jesus Zendejas runs the pruning and picking crews. "People like working for him, so when we get into pruning he's got 20 people asking him to hire them, so he can get the three that he wants." The rest of the crew are Jose Medina, Ignacio Sanchez, Pablo Andrade, Jerry Simmons and Jeremy Gardner, field workers.

Calera still keeps its winery and vineyard crews separate. Ryan's men don't work in the winery, and the cellarmen hardly ever visit the vineyards. Jensen tried mixing crews once, getting the vineyard men to come down off the mountain to help when the grapes were in, but it didn't work. The crews resisted each other; there were turf problems, personality clashes. The vine-yard workers are, in his words, "sort of ornery mountain men," and they prefer the freedom of working out in the fields. "Not every operation is run that way, but ours is because there's so much physical distance between the two. The vineyard guys get the grapes to the winery hoppers, and that's it."

When my picture-taking was over on that first visit, I walked back to my car, parked on the upper-level road. It was late afternoon and a breeze like soft skin drifted across the landscape. It smelled of windblown dust and wild rosemary, with a faint trace of blue-gum eucalyptus, elusive and tantalizing. There was a beetle at the side of the road, its head down, butting at a small pebble, its black carapace gleaming in the slanting sun, its purpose inscrutable – *what will it do with the pebble when it gets it up the hill?* I looked back over the winery's angular roof to the landscape beyond, to the lengthening shadows on the distant slopes, black clefts in the golden hills. I felt a sudden slight melancholic tugging. It looked and smelled of home, of the hills between Fransch Hoek, where my heart is, and the golden fields of De Aar, where the African plains begin, the endless North which only ends in the Great Thirstland of the Kalahari Desert. Somewhere below, on the Cienaga Road, a dog barked, and I thought I could faintly hear the lowing of cattle. In 2006 we parked our car on the lower level, but before we drove away I looked out over that same magnificent view, then up at the angular winery above. In its cellars were maybe 20,000 cases of wine, pinot noir and chardonnay, viognier and a small test batch of Aligoté, Central Coast wines and a blend Jensen just called Mélange. In there, under the care of the Corona brothers, waiting for their time to be shipped and taxed and consumed, were some of the best wines being made anywhere on the planet. As we drove off, the slanting sun caught a crag a dozen miles away in a sudden golden flare, and at the gate a bobcat snarled at the passing car. A grand place, I thought, an appropriate place for a great wine and a grand obsession.

CHAPTER THREE

In which the pinot noir makes its
appearance as the heartbreak grape
and some thought is given to where
it came from and where it's going

When it comes right down to it, all winemaking is similar – it's the process of helping grapes ferment themselves into wine.

But, clearly, some methods of encouraging this process are better than others. And some grapes make the job easier than others.

The pinot noir is one of the more difficult ones.

In those innocent days when gender descriptives were still thought amusing, the pinot noir was called feminine – by which was meant flighty, changeable, capricious, beguiling and seductive.

In the same vein, they called it the heartbreak grape because it was so stubborn, so particular, so elusive, so damn difficult to get right. And also because when it was at its best it made the most sublime wine of all. The heartbreak grape? You cannot break a heart without having captured it first.

The greatest wines of Burgundy, which is where the greatest pinot noirs have traditionally been elevated, are tantalizing, elusive, poetic, thrilling. Even the most inspired red Bordeaux, that cunning mixture of cabernet and merlot, can't fill the head with spiced dreams quite like the great Burgundies. No other red wine can balance spice and fruit so . . . flirtatiously, can seem at once so ripe and fragile, so decadent and clean, so irresistible. And, it's fair to say, no other red wines can drive the poor writer to such extravagant prolixity, as you can plainly see from the foregoing, or from this overblown passage from Oz Clarke: "The flavours of the great red Burgundies are sensuous, often erotic, above rational discourse and beyond the powers of measured criticism as they flout the conventions in favour of something rooted in emotions and passions too powerful to be taught, too ancient to be meddled with."

Whew!

The heartbreak comes from dim memories of this greatness as producers all over the world, from the valleys of California or New Zealand to the hearty plains of Australia or Argentina, contemplate the thin, mean and insipid wines they have managed to concoct out of the blessed pinot noir. If truth be told, many of the most insipid come only a few metres from the great *domaines* of Burgundy itself, from lesser slopes or lesser soil or lesser growers and producers taking lesser care. And equal heartbreak from contemplation of attempts in California to make wines approximating The Big Red One, heavy, stultifying wines tasting of burned plum or, in the words of Jancis Robinson, wines that "smelled unnervingly of burned cabbage."

The capricious nature of pinot noir in the bottle reflects a similar flightiness in the vine itself. Pinot noir mutates if you give it a cross look, seemingly out of pure spite. It's a master of the genetic dance. It's also very old, and no one can any longer say which is the "original" clone; there was pinot noir already planted in the Burgundy area soon after the Romans pushed gingerly into the deep interior of Gaul – Pliny describes it, in an early bout of critical purple. And Burgundy is now thick with clones of all qualities, after many attempts to fight off the viruses and funguses to which the variety is so prone, blast it. Some "burgundies" are made with what probably isn't pinot noir at all, but *pinot droit*, an upright clone similar to many invented in California by the techies of Davis, which bears more fruit than the traditional *pinot fin*. There are supposed to be 365 "clones" of pinot noir now growing along the tight little ridge of Burgundy. Well, that's a neat number – others say there are 200, or 1,000. And, considering that each clone would affect the wine differently because of its particular genetic structure, it's easy to see why this is "a minx of a vine," an exasperating variety for growers, winemakers and critics, as well as the humble wine drinker. This welter of wines, this passel of pinots, makes standard-bearing and standard-keeping a thankless task. It's further complicated by the pinot noir vine's tendency to degenerate and to die early, sometimes decades before it should. And complicated yet again by pinot noir's notorious reluctance to travel to new climes, where its "feminine" allure seems to pine away into old-maidish rectitude.

That, at least, was the thought a decade or so ago. The problem was, winemakers in these "new climes" got it all wrong. They plunked the vine down into the arid heat of the

California plains, where the poor thing became sunburned and petulant. As a consequence, the early American pinot noirs had size and weight, but lacked subtlety, finesse, or much character.

If that wasn't enough, the pinot noir is also an early budder with sluggish secondary growth, so spring frosts are deadly. Some years the vines stubbornly refuse to set fruit, the flowers simply withering instead of turning to precious grapes. No one seems to know why.

The pinot noir grape is as capricious as the vine. Its petulance comes from its thin skin. It needs – demands – regular sun to ripen, but will quickly overripen if the sun gets too hot. On the other hand, it can't cope with too much rain. It will swell and burst and rot if it gets too wet at harvest time. It's also an early ripener; the longer the grapes can stay on the vine, the more complex the resulting wines, but the tendencies to rot in the rain and to burn in the sun greatly elevate the risk. And if it gets too ripe it will lose its fruit flavours and potential for grandeur.

Colour, flavours and tannins are precariously balanced in the pinot noir. Sometimes, the vine seems naturally to produce grapes rich in tannins and anthocyanins and a deep ruby colour. More often, it will produce an insipid rosé the colour of antique brick. Climate can effect this swing. So can weather, soil, elevation, sunshine, moisture, pruning, picking, fermentation, filtering and a dozen other things, apparently up to and including the phases of the moon and the moods of the winemaker.

To the wine drinker, pinot noirs are robust, vigorous and explosive. But to the winemaker, they are fragile, prone to spoilage, delicate and capricious. The making of pinot noir requires a deftness of touch that was generally thought to be alien to the Californian character. Got an A-plus in enological studies? The pinot noir won't care. As Steve Doerner once put it, "Since pinot noir starts out as a delicate wine without a strong backbone, every time you do something to it, you strip more of the body out of it. So, if you're striving for a rich, complex wine, the less you handle it, the closer you'll come." With pinot noir, structure is easy to get. It is subtleness, perfume and richness that are the difficult things. Because of this . . . elusiveness . . . the making of pinot noir becomes an overriding passion and obsession. Its nature remains a mystery, and it remains the wine that most serious winemakers want to make – and most serious winemakers want to drink.

And there's one other problem with it. It changes, capriciously, and often, even in the bottle. Josh Jensen, when he's holding a tasting for important clients, likes to open a bottle the night before to see how it's "performing." This is not a matter of variation between bottles of the same batch, which plagues all winemakers, but that pinot noir is always restless, constantly undergoing changes, cyclical – but cyclical in an unknown and unknowable periodicity.

So while everyone recognizes a great pinot noir when they come across one, pinot noir has no single universally accepted flavour or style. It can be pitiful to watch wine writers struggling for acceptable comparatives. Without trying, you can find pinot noir variously tasting of fresh wild strawberries (or, more often, raspberries), of damsons or other plums, of black cherries, of vanilla and butter and violets on the delicate side, of pepper and all-spice and truffles on the robust side and of "earthiness," sometimes off-puttingly described as "farmyard" or "barnyard" or game, or even rotten vegetables. One eminent writer, despairingly, wrote that it "smelled like shit," and meant it, approvingly. Of course, presumably she meant the sweeter odour of the cow, and she was likely thinking of hay in a summer barn, but I still think she should have tried again.

Joseph Ward, writing in *Condé Nast Traveler* in September 1992, said of pinot noir that it was "quicksilver to cabernet's iron," a nice phrase. Joel Fleishman, wine *amateur* and sometime university president, waxed embarrassingly poetic in *Vanity Fair* in August 1991: "At their best, pinot noirs are the most romantic of wines, with so voluptuous a perfume, so sweet an edge, and so powerful a punch that, like falling in love, they make the blood run hot and the soul wax embarrassingly poetic." (Well, at least he admitted it.)

The great California winemaker André Tchelistcheff, who can be forgiven the solecism because of his old-fashioned European courtliness, once called pinot noir "the wonderful aroma of the inside of a kid glove worn by a young woman." This will not do much for its marketing among female drinkers, but unreconstructed romantic males can see what he means.

Could pinot noir be made to work in California? Tchelistcheff, always good for a quote, once said he'd made a "superb pinot noir [at Beaulieu in Napa], but I don't know how I did it and I was never able to do it again."

Until the late 1980s, most California pinot noirs are still hot and simplistic, one-dimensional wines; when you heard a California winemaker defend himself by saying he was trying for "a California style," you could be sure he meant he was unable to duplicate what he knew in his heart was the real thing. Still, this defensiveness was forgivable. For years Californians smarted from the condescension of the lofty

Burgundians. That the French, secure in their centuries-old Gallic superiority, were able to be snottily polite, only made it worse – the French have always been able to say "yes, but ..." better than anyone. Typical was the haughty Lalou Leroy, co-proprietor of the mighty Domaine de la Romanée-Conti, who, when confronted with a superb pinot noir from Chalone, sniffed, "*Oui, mais c'est chaud.*" She later deigned to be "impressed" by Oregon and remembered an Eyrie Vineyards pinot noir that was "*interessant . . . mais assez leger.*"

Well, this is all gone now. Madame may sniff, but the more foresighted Burgundians are sending their sons to America and Australia to learn the new ways of doing things. Just as the Californians and the Oregonians learned a hard-won lesson: Go back to Burgundy to see how it's done.

In the early years of the new millennium the problems were oddly similar, though in some ways reversed.

It was true that there were splendid pinot noirs being made, by Josh Jensen, of course, and his confreres in the now-defunct pinot noir Producers Association, Acacia (Chalone), Zaca Mesa, Sanford, Belvedere, Iron Horse, Château Bouchaine and others, who were all producing wines as rich and as satisfying as the best of the Old World, wines that smelled of cherries and ripe plums, of chocolate and leather, with the same beguiling sweet silk of the greatest red Burgundies, those of the Domaine de la Romanée-Conti, or those of Henri Jayer in Vosne-Romanée and Nuits-St.-George. But – many of the newer California pinot noirs were again overly alcoholic, too dense, "jammy," with too much fruit and not enough finesse. The difference was in the attitude. There was no longer any defensiveness, only bravado. They were actually trying for these overblown (or opulent if your views were more benign) wines; they actually wanted wines with nearly 15 per cent alcohol, a dense beetroot in colour, as though pinot should resemble a mourvèdre or something from the lower Rhône. And they had become unbecomingly scornful of Burgundy – and by extension Calera – with its obsession for complexity and subtlety. How much of this was the fault of Robert Parker and his ilk was a lively debate among Old World devotees in 2006.

Our bottle of wine – any bottle of wine – can have its lineage tracked to ancient times, thousands of generations of producers and consumers. No one knows how far back the vine goes. Brillat-Savarin, the gourmet and critic, is typical of many in France who assume that wine was made in the far mists of time. "There are only two things that separate man from the beasts," he wrote: "Fear of the future, and a desire for fermented liquors." Wine is mentioned in many texts of ancient Mesopotamia, of ancient Egypt, and of Gaul. The *Epic of Gilgamesh* has many stanzas singing the praises of wine; so does the *Song of Solomon*. There were vineyards in Sumeria, in Assyria and in ancient Greece. Primitive grape presses, fermentation tanks and treading platforms antedating Christ by millennia have been found in the Caucasus between the Black and Caspian seas. From there it's fair to say that the Caucasians, wherever they went, took grapevines with them. From what we now call Syria and Lebanon the Phoenicians distributed grapes throughout the Mediterranean. So did their successors, the Greeks, who, upon first being exposed to Italy, called it the Land of Vines, the same name given by the Vikings to North America two thousand years later, when confronted with the native *Vitis labrusca* (with which, alas, they attempted to make wine – and still do, in places, producing gallons of mediocre, highly coloured wine with a pronounced flavour, rather mysteriously called "foxy" by wine people). The vine arrived in France more than two thousand years ago from the Transcaucasus by way of the Euphrates valley, Egypt and Greece. Probably the colonizers from ancient Ionia first grew grapes at the mouth of the Rhône, but it was the Romans who first planted vines in the interior of "that barbarous place." And after the collapse of the Roman Empire, the wine business was essentially saved by the Christians, who needed it for their Mass; monastic Christian orders were among the first to set out vineyards in what are now some of the most highly regarded wine-growing regions of Germany, France, Austria and the Danube Valley.

The California wine industry which began in the 1870s, induced largely by Italian and East European immigrants, proved short-lived – rye whisky was still the American alcoholic beverage of choice. The years following the repeal of Prohibition produced little wine of interest, though Davis was quietly doing its work, and the Gallos were laying the foundation for their extraordinary dominance of American winemaking. It wasn't until the 1970s that California noticed that it was producing wines of great character and complexity in numerous small pockets around the state – the Russian River Valley, the Green Valley, Napa and Sonoma and Santa Barbara and Monterey, though the chilly fogs in Monterey Bay made it hard to ripen grapes. And in the late 1970s, with the famous Paris Tasting that pitted the best Americans against the best Europeans, to Europe's chagrin and America's triumph, the world at last accepted California as one of the premier wine regions on the planet.

They made wonderful robust cabernets. They produced merlots, chardonnays, sauvignon blancs, even zinfandels of quality. Only the pinot noir eluded them. By the end of the '70s the Heartbreak Grape was still regarded as the Last Hurdle for California winemakers.

Vitis vinifera is only one of about 40 grape species in the world. Almost all of them are deciduous, highly susceptible to fungi and parasites, needful of considerable heat and sunlight and – perhaps most importantly – able to cross-breed spontaneously. There are now literally thousands of vinifera varieties and, if you count clones, as the viticulturalists call stable mutations, thousands more.

You can make wines from all of them. Poor wines, mostly. Only a handful, fewer than 50, of the great vinifera catalogue will make wines worth drinking. But what a litany of names! The chardonnay, gamay and pinot noir of Burgundy. The sauvignons, cabernet and blanc, of Bordeaux. The sangiovese and the sublime nebbiolo of Italy. The riesling of Germany, the chenin blanc of the Loire and the viognier and grenache of the Rhône. The sémillon, which makes the silken sweetness of sauternes; the muscat of the Crimea and southern Spain – I have a particular fondness for the muscat, because from it my ancestors made the succulent sweet wine called Constantia, which was drunk to much acclaim at the court of Napoleon.

In much of the wine-growing world grape varieties have been matched to *terroir*, as the French call their little micro-pockets, over the centuries. In many places, such as Bordeaux, no one variety will do and a blend has been found to do best. Few in the Old World ever listed the grape varieties on their labels, which seemed designed rather to satisfy local pride and parochial politics than enlighten the drinker. Nor was it strictly necessary. Everyone in the region already knew what the grape variety was. And, later, it was mandated by law – you can't call a white burgundy by that name unless it's made entirely of chardonnay. Therefore, while the wines were well known, few consumers knew the grape. Who had heard of the palomino of sherry, the syrah and the elegant, flowery viognier of the Rhône, the merlot, malbec and petit verdot of Bordeaux or, until recently, the gewürztraminer of Alsace? It was only in the New World that winemakers, no longer bound by tradition (because tradition, by definition, is accreted and not invented), began to label their wines with the grape varietal. The Old World is now following suit (the new trendiness of viognier in California, for instance, has persuaded the handful of French producers to declare its existence on their labels too), and this has done more to simplify the pleasures of wine than almost anything else.

There's still plenty of room for disagreement among ampelographers, grape specialists. America's zinfandel is the most prominent example – is it really a primitivo from Italy, or something else entirely? Is Spain's pedro ximenez, used for making sherry, really a riesling from Germany? Does anyone but the nationalist zealots care?

The Romans were wine drinkers and arbiters of taste, and established the vineyards that still endure as the greatest in France: on the low spit of gravel, limestone and clay between the Atlantic and the Gironde near Bordeaux, on the chalky hills of champagne, in the flinty Loire valley, and in Burgundy, on an undistinguished and commonplace limestone ridge less than 30 kilometres long, called the Côte d'Or, which is remarkable only for its unremarkableness. Still, the Côte d'Or is the heart of Burgundy, and has produced wines of superlative quality. Samuel Johnson was one of many wine drinkers who fell in love with the wines of this small ridge. Years later he confided that he couldn't remember much about the first time he had made love; he couldn't remember the date or the woman's name, and could only faintly picture her face and her body. "But the wine! The wine, by god, was a Chambertin!" (My own view of this anecdote, having read contemporary descriptions of Johnson, was that the Chambertin was the only reason the young woman agreed to be seduced in the first place.)

An even more remarkable thing about this unremarkable ridge is the fact that some few small parcels on its slopes yield up superlative wines, and others do not, and though soil and subsoil and temperature and humidity and *climat* – the elevation above the fogs, the aspect or slope of the parcel, its orientation towards the sun and the prevailing winds – have all been exhaustively analyzed, the central mystery remains. With one more added: two growers on the same parcel will make very different wines.

Burgundy and Bordeaux winemaking differ not only because of grape varieties and climate, but also because of history and politics. The reason many Bordeaux wines are produced on substantial estates is because Eleanor of Aquitaine, when she held the region, imposed on it the English system of primogeniture. The estate generally went to the eldest son, and so was kept intact. By contrast, although Burgundy was once one of the greatest duchies of France, it was broken up by the last of the Bourbon kings and its remaining great landholdings, those of the church, were scattered by

Napoleon. As a result, it now has a curiously rustic air – there are none of the great châteaux of the Loire here, nor even the great merchant houses so prominent along the Médoc. Instead, there has been endless subdivision of land. It's still common-place for four sons to inherit a small property, each to jealously guard his half hectare. For a grower in Burgundy, three acres is a large property, and it would be larger than most of his neighbours.

Therefore, the Burgundians have attempted a complex grading of fields; each field, and even each part of a field, has been classified and inserted into a hierarchy that is codified and cast into law. There are a hundred or more appellations in Burgundy, many of them referring to a minute parcel of a specific vineyard, and built into these allowable appellations is a classification by quality (into Grands Crus, Premiers Crus, Appellations Communales and, at the bottom, simply Bourgogne). The differences on the label can be minute, but the variance in quality absolute. Many villages, for reasons of status and therefore income, have attached their names to famous vineyards, and the results can be confusing and apparently contradictory – Chassagne-Montrachet can be wine of varying quality from anywhere in a big commune; Chevalier-Montrachet can only be wine from one tiny, if famous, vineyard. Nor can the human factor be codified. A wine from a particular field in a particular commune in a particular year could still have been made by any of six or seven winemakers. Monopoles, or whole vineyards in the hands of one grower, are rare exceptions. Of those "monopoles," the 1.8 hectares of the Domaine de la Romanée-Conti is the most prestigious, and the wines produced there, Romanée-Conti, La Tâche, Richebourg, and Romanée-St.-Vivant, are the most coveted red wines in the world, now fetching prices out of reach of all but the very wealthy or the completely besotted. The vines are perfectly sited in limestone soil above the village of Vosne-Romanée, but this doesn't begin to explain the extraordinary opulence, the velvety warmth, the complexity and spiciness of the wines.

Romanée-Conti has always been the model, the grail, for Josh Jensen. On that monopole lies the real origin of our bottle, in reality as well as fancy, as we shall see.

Burgundian styles vary too, and have varied over time. Historically, they were deep and dark. About 15 years ago there was a swing to much lighter wines, paler, with less depth of flavour and less ability to mature; and after a few years, the start of another swing, back to richness and complexity. These cycles have continued: Burgundy has not been immune to the hectoring of the *Wine Advocate*, Robert Parker's newsletter, and briefly flirted at the start of this century with an almost Californian opulence, what Josh Jensen calls "sledgehammer wines." Mercifully, the flirtation was brief and Burgundian sanity has been restored. Josh Jensen's view remains that of the classic Burgundian: the perfect pinot noir is one that is perfectly balanced on the cusp of richness and complexity, of fruitiness and subtlety, and is neither one nor the other. It should be light and delicate as well as opulent, and complex and subtle above all.

There are other complications to understanding Burgundy. Burgundian winemakers are not usually, or even typically, grape growers, although that is changing fast as the growers challenge the power of the merchants of Beaune, called *négociants*.

Traditionally, most of Burgundy's growers were farmers

who grew the grapes and pressed them, and in the musty depths of their old cellar basements they'd keep 10 or 11 barrels, where they'd store the new raw wine. Then Louis Latour or Joseph Drouhin or one of the Jaffelin Frères or another of the great *négociants* would come by and taste it, and if they liked it and met the farmer's price they'd buy it from him, all his barrels of raw newly fermented wine. If his patch was entitled to the name Chevry Chambertin Grand Cru, then along with the barrels the merchant would get the green tags that allowed him to bottle and sell that many bottles of Chevry Chambertin.

In the last 20 years this has been changing. The 1980s brought a horrid inflation in the prices of Burgundies. As prices on the open market soared, criticism swelled also – criticism of the poor quality of much of the wine. The powerful backlash that resulted persuaded some of the younger growers – and a few older ones – to assert themselves. They wanted a better living for themselves, and to produce something they could be proud of. They began to call themselves "harvesting proprietors," and began to finish the winemaking themselves, marketing and selling their own produce. As a consequence, the great and arrogant *négociants* lost considerable power, and in some years, much to the malicious glee of the growers, they now actually have trouble getting enough juice. All this has made good Burgundy harder and harder to find and buy, but cheaper and more interesting because of it.

And one more thing happened: as California began to produce better wines, the small Burgundians, lacking the prejudices of their betters, began to understand that there was now real competition coming from the New World. The best ones welcomed it; the others whined.

The Californians, for their part, moved closer to the older sensibility of Burgundy. As Josh Jensen put it, "There are many growers who don't make wine here. In fact, most California wine comes from farmers who sell their crop to whoever comes along, to five different wineries if those wineries pay their price. We at Calera do that with our Central Coast wines, which in the drought years have been as much as 80 per cent of our production. We try to find some good pinot noir and chardonnay vineyards and just buy their fruit."

But his heart isn't there. "I'm a Burgundian. That's my perspective. Control of grapes, the climate from which they come and the soil in which they are grown, is paramount to me. I must have my own vineyards to make great wine."

CHAPTER FOUR

In which the maker of our bottle
of wine goes to Burgundy to pick
grapes and to learn some
pre-19th-century technology

The man who made our bottle of wine grew up across the Bay from San Francisco. His mother's family owned a lumbering company in the Pacific Northwest; his father, Stephen Fairchild Jensen, was born in Seattle in 1910 and paid his way through dental school by driving trucks for his cousins' Seattle seafood company. He was, from all accounts, a better dentist than truck driver; his most vivid moment as a trucker came when he failed to make a turn one frosty morning, spilling a truckload of fresh oysters over Highway 99.

Before the war he practised dentistry for a number of years in Beijing, where he married and raised Josh's older brother and sister. After a stint in the Navy, he set up his dental practice in the Bay Area town of Orinda. Along the way he fished and hunted, bred black Labrador hunting dogs and, with his wife, raised quarter horses.

Wine, however, was never part of the household's daily life; it was never served with meals, and the family had no cellar, and stored what few bottles they acquired in their Quonset hut barn, along with the cow, horses and a pig – much to the amusement of Dr. George Selleck, who had given them the wine.

It was Selleck, a dentist colleague and friend of Jensen *père*, who first introduced young Josh to wine, and could be said to be the founding father of our bottle. Jensen recalls him with affection: "It was in the late 1940s that George thought my dad should start learning about wine and bought him some German wines. It was these my dad stored in our Quonset hut. I remember tasting them with George. He had a major collection of wine, a great cellar, and with it an incredible palate for and knowledge of wine. He was a connoisseur of the first rank, a man who knew everyone in the wine business in California. Later, at dinners at his house, I progressed to Bordeaux and Burgundies."

It was Selleck who first pointed out to young Josh that the wine world could be divided into two distinct and irreconcilable factions, passionate Bordelais and romantic Burgundians, though Selleck himself could (and did) swing both ways, and had wonderful collections of each.

He was one of the founders of the San Francisco Food & Wine Society, and was the first dentist president of the Society of Medical Friends of Wine. In the '40s and '50s he served as one of five judges at the California State Fair Wine Competition, then the only competition of any consequence in America. The other four judges were André Tchelistcheff,

Philip Wagner, the winemaker and author from the East Coast, the eminent Professor Maynard Amerine of UC Davis and Dr. Salvatore Lucia of San Francisco.

Amerine once told Josh about a blind tasting hosted by another member of their group of post-Prohibition San Francisco wine pioneers, in which everyone was given eight glasses of red wine and asked to identify them. The host appeared to have stumped them when, as Amerine recounted it, George suddenly got that twinkle in his eye, retasted the eight glasses, and wrote out his guesses. He alone recognized that it was all Château Latour, eight different vintages, and he correctly identified six of the eight. Amerine believed it one of the greatest feats of blind tasting he'd ever seen.

Selleck was twice decorated by the French government, as Chevalier du Merite Agricole, and Commandeur du Merite Agricole, for his knowledge of French wine and food. "He was a true connoisseur and bon vivant in the best sense of both terms, and his joie de vivre, expertise and generosity were and remain an inspiration for me," Jensen wrote in a memorial much later.

Josh put in a few years at Yale and then went to Oxford to do a master's in anthropology, for reasons he now forgets – little of what he learned there stuck with him, except, for our purposes, his further education into the mysteries of Burgundy.

He spent more time, in truth, in a boat than a classroom. Although bigger than the norm for an oarsman, he did make the Oxford team and competed in the annual Boat Race against Cambridge at Henley, earning himself a mention in the *Guinness Book of Records* as the heaviest man ever to have done so. He enjoyed rowing, and the Oxford team of the time, unusually, stayed together and competed in a Grand Challenge international event, eventually losing in the semi-finals to the East Germans.

Oxford was the first time in his life he drank wine on an everyday basis. Not necessarily in college, though at every Oxford college there's a High Table at which the faculty and heads of college eat and drink wines from formidable cellars. Jensen was not High Table material, but there were plenty of good restaurants around the city, and he could afford to eat out frequently. Much later, at a Vinexpo show in Bordeaux, Jensen met the eminent Jean Michel Cazes, a star in the wine business, proprietor of Château Lynch Bages and the manager and operator of a number of other Bordeaux wineries. "I told him that when I was a student at Oxford, Lynch Bages was my regular dinner wine, and he was pretty surprised. But then, in a restaurant, you'd maybe pay seven or eight dollars, or ten, for a bottle of Lynch Bages or its equivalent. In the sixties, you really could drink those wines. You didn't need to be a millionaire to drink great wines. Wine was just an everyday thing. (He didn't tell Cazes that Lynch Bages was known as "Lunch Buckets" to generations of Oxford students.)

"I don't really remember when the light went on, but on it clicked, and suddenly I realized, hey, wine is a part of life, not just something you have at Christmas dinner or when you put a tuxedo on. It's part of the richness of everyday life."

It was there, at Oxford, and Château Lunch Buckets notwithstanding, that he gave his heart to Burgundy.

"I was at Oxford for two and a half years, and I suppose that during that time I had wine every night with dinner. And after a while, I found that I liked the ones called Chevry Chambertin and Nuits St. George, or Vosne-Romanée, more than I liked the ones called Château this or Château that.

"I love a great Bordeaux. When I have a great Bordeaux I say to myself, this is a great wine, this has everything, colour, intensity, flavour, balance, acid. But when I taste a great Burgundy I say wow, I'm in love! It's very different. It's a visceral, emotional response. And I've seen Bordelais react the same way, but in reverse."

He was still pretty hazy on the geography of Burgundy, but not at all hazy in knowing that the academic life was not for him. He didn't want to be a professor. So he set off for the Côte d'Or.

"I knew I really liked drinking the wine. I wanted to see if I liked the life, the work, the elbow-grease end of it. Could I make my life doing this?"

He set off in the summer of 1969.

He knew the language, sort of. "I'd taken French at school and college for five years, so I could read and write beautifully. But I couldn't speak it. I couldn't order a cup of coffee properly – that's part of the teaching of languages in this country, at least back then. So I learned to speak by living there."

Where was "there"?

George Selleck had shared a few precious bottles of Romanée-Conti with the young Jensen, and had told him something of the lore and the prestige of the place, "So I knew that was the best place to learn winemaking – why not go for the very best there is? So I simply went there, I showed up one day and knocked on the door. Do you need pickers? I asked.

"Yeah, they said, come back in about a week, what's your name?

"They seemed quite surprised to see me. They didn't have a lot of Americans volunteering to pick grapes."

The great *domaines* of Burgundy draw their field workers from several sources. The harvest in Burgundy is in September, stretching through to October, and the first pickers are French students, who do it to make a little cash; they start in the south, in Provence, and follow the harvest north, Burgundy being one of the last, before Champagne. The second source of help is people from the surrounding villages, wives of the workers, wives of the cellarmen, neighbours. This is the traditional source of all harvest labour. The third source is people who simply love the work. Josh Jensen remembers a fellow picker at Romanée-Conti in 1970 who worked in a bank in Dijon. "He took his vacation every year at harvest time, and worked like a pig all through harvest. I still remember this 30 years later, it astonished me so much, because that is hard, hard work. It's often cold and raining, but he loved it. It was a great change for him." The fourth source is gypsy, the Roma of Europe. "They're the equivalent of our Mexicans, immigrant migrant field workers. These guys work so fast! You try to put a student with soft hands out there and these guys will be at the end of the row before the student has picked the first two vines." Jensen himself was part of a small but not unimpressive fifth category – students of the business.

Even in the high-margin wineries of the Grands Crus, the harvest, the *vendange*, is not at all a grim industrial occasion; Burgundy, after all, has been known as the stomach of France, and picking is an occasion for merriment and singing, festivity and food. The winery lodges and feeds its pickers, who take their meals in the fields, weather permitting. Breakfasts can be sardines, bread and red wine. Lunch is pot au feu or a cassoulet, soups, fish dishes, with pots of red wine, bread and great hunks of cheese.

Jensen was hired at the Domaine de la Romanée-Conti by one of the great figures of French winemaking, the *maître de chai* of the *domaine*, André Noblet. Noblet presided over the winemaking at Romanée-Conti for many years, a great, hulking bear of a figure (he had been a prominent rugby player as a youth) with twinkling eyes and a shrewd appreciation of man and nature. He had wanted to be a printer, but was persuaded back to the calling of his father by M. Leroy, the unbending proprietor of Romanée-Conti. When Josh first met him he was near the end of his long career, but at the height of his knowledge and authority. He'd been born in the village itself, knew everyone, had the confidence of his employers, made the best wines in the world – he was perfectly placed to teach the young Californian what he needed to know.

"The really nice thing about the best wineries," Jensen recalls, "is that they're like the best chefs. They really don't have secrets. It always bugs me when I hear someone ask a chef, how did you make this sauce? And he says, 'that's a secret.' Those are the small individuals with little knowledge and small talent, because they're afraid they won't be able to stay ahead of their competitors. The real talents are happy to share all they know, because they know that next year they'll be creating something new and even better. They're teachers. André Noblet was very much like that."

Not everyone in Burgundy, however, was "like that," and Jensen ran afoul of French xenophobia in his second harvest as a picker at Romanée-Conti.

"After the '70 crush was over I told André I'd like to work in the cellar for the following harvest, and then go back to the States.

"Sure, he said, no problem.

"I pushed him: Do you have to ask anybody else about this?

"And he said, No, I'm the *maître de chai* and I don't have to ask anybody.

"I checked with him four times during the year – I *can* work in the cellar, right? I'd learned what I could in the vineyard. And the first year I'd hung around for a week after the harvest, picking up what I could. Also, in the mornings before we went into the fields I'd help punch down the fermenting cap in the tanks. It's called the *pigeage*, and you do it with your feet in the old way, you just get into the tank and push the cap down. There had been a huge crop that year, and they'd de-stemmed the bunches just for space reasons – mostly they fermented their wines with all the stems attached. This punching down is hard work. I'd help in the morning and then, after we'd finished the picking, I'd help with the evening punch-down too, asking questions all the time, learning, and André liked this. I was a good worker.

"So I showed up for the '71 harvest and reported to the cellar as planned. And there I ran afoul of one of the members of one of the families that owned, and still owns, Romanée-Conti. The *domaine* is owned by two families, the de Villaine family, whose visible person of my generation is Aubert, a friend of mine since those days, and the Leroy family. The second or third day I was in the cellar shovelling grapes into tanks and punching down and doing other cellar work, and I spotted old M. de Villaine, Aubert's father, and old M. Leroy talking. Aubert and Leroy's daughter, Lalou, were called in and were casting nervous glances in my direction. Finally, to his embarrassment, they sent Aubert over to tell me that M. Leroy didn't want me in the winery.

"I said I'd checked with André a dozen times, but it was no use.

"I'm sorry, Aubert said, he just doesn't want you here. He wants you in the fields.

"I don't do fields, I said. I did that last year.

"I went on working.

"Then Lalou came over. We think you should go out in the fields, she said.

"I don't think so, no thank you, I said.

"Finally her father came over and said, 'Well, we think you'd be better off in the fields.'

"If I can't work here in the cellar I'm not working for you in this harvest, I said.

"Well, sorry you feel that way, he said.

"Okay, I'll check out right away, I said, and I went to my friend's place. It was pretty uncomfortable. But out I went."

Jensen has maintained friendly relations with Aubert de Villaine ever since, but never warmed to the remarkable Lalou, one of the great characters of Burgundy. "I've preferred to stay in a different room; I'd rather not have anything to do with her."

Lalou, meanwhile, went on to become the public face of the DRC, as Romanée-Conti is known to the trade; she was, among others things, its official sales agent. Lalou was (and is), to put it politely, a forceful personality. She was often seen in the *chai* in her chic trousers and smart little bomber jackets, issuing orders hither and yon. But she knew her stuff: Gault & Millau, the French restaurant critics, have written of her encyclopedic knowledge of wines (though their judgment might have been coloured by the meals she served to France's gastronomic elite, including themselves, every year – perhaps her friendship with the great chef Jean Troisgros didn't hurt either). It was always assumed that Lalou bullied the quiet and scholarly Aubert, though she used to say of him, "We take all the important decisions together, although we don't always agree." As it happens, Jensen picked the right person for a friend: Lalou, otherwise known as Mme Bize-Leroy, was fired as DRC's sales agent after a long legal wrangle and wound up on the losing side of a $12-million lawsuit against the property and the de Villaine family. She has since set up her own winery, under the name Leroy, and its wines are highly praised in the wine press. By the public, too, apparently; she prices them aggressively and you'd need better than $400 to pick up a bottle.

Jensen is still puzzled why he was ejected. It wasn't for the "secrets" – even had there been any, André Noblet would tell them to all and sundry. "I think it was difficult, and different, for them to have an American come over. They didn't have any secrets, it wasn't that. They just didn't want anyone poking around."

In a way, Jensen had already learned what he needed. Not so much in the fields, but afterwards. The pickers never got to drink DRC wines. They would eat and drink endlessly – hunks of bread, hunks of cheese, hunks of sausage and a big tub of wine, "so we'd been drinking wine all day long to mellow out while we were picking in the rain." This was wine they made specifically for the pickers at harvest time, at its best merely acceptable.

Despite the mellowness, Jensen managed anyway, through André's courtesy.

"By the time I left I'd learned quite a bit by watching. And because André couldn't speak English, and the DRC would get a lot of American business people coming through, André would bring me out to translate. And while I was translating, I was tasting. When André got some big shots in for a tasting he'd haul them all out – he'd taste all the barrels of one vintage and then all the barrels of the next, and then he'd start bringing out the bottles. The retailers from New Jersey would ask, what date did they pick this? When did they do that? And I'd ask André and translate, and meantime I'd get to taste and taste and taste these wines, these sublime wines, and I'd be learning all the time."

Between the '70 and the '71 vintages Jensen was either living in Paris or travelling through Bordeaux, up to Champagne, down the Rhône valley, and back to Burgundy. He'd spend time in Burgundy, and would stop by to see André and be asked to do another translation, and have a taste of this or that *domaine* wine.

He picked for a while at the Domaine Dujac, whose owner, Jacques Seysses, became one of his closest friends, and in nearby Condrieu on the Rhône, where he was paid in bottles of viognier wine. "You can't in any case survive financially picking grapes. I was using some money I inherited. I wasn't staying at five star hotels either. I stayed with friends a lot. My car was a Citroën Deux Chevaux delivery van. It cost me $40. I drove it for a year and sold it for $40 at the end. But I did spend good money at restaurants. At that time for $20 you could have a good meal for one person in most three star restaurants."

He'd already bought all the French wine texts, particularly the Burgundy texts, and was plowing through them to figure out what else he needed to know to actually make the kinds of wine he liked to drink.

"I'd pretty much decided by then. I liked the work, I liked

the people, I liked the product, I liked the art of it, I liked the challenge of trying to make something that everybody at that time said just could not be done in the U.S. I was *ready*."

What he learned was a style of winemaking that he was to take back to the United States, there to find himself in complete opposition to the prevailing American mode, which was high-tech, dominated by chemists. When he first went to Burgundy he'd been shocked at how little processing or handling was done to the grapes. "I mean, basically they pick the grapes and they put them in tanks, and then they go away for a couple of days, and then they come back to see if it's started fermenting yet." He kept looking around eagerly, waiting for the magic procedures, the great secrets, the enological legerdemain, to begin. "But there was no hocus pocus. And here's the secret: the making of great pinot noir is like making a Model T Ford, just a few simple steps.

"These are the greatest wines in the world, and they are made by the most bare-bones production methods – grapes, wooden casks, bottles. Not even a filter, never mind a centrifuge. This wasn't space-age technology. It wasn't even 19th-century technology.

"I was absolutely entranced."

A few months later, Jensen went home to make our bottle of wine.

CHAPTER FIVE

*In which our winemaker returns
to California to apply what he
has learned and buys an eyedropper
and a bottle of hydrochloric acid*

Josh Jensen returned to California in 1973 ready, as he put it, "to go for broke," to begin the adventure, to start making the great wine he knew he was capable of. His nostrils, and his dreams, were filled with the aromas of great Burgundian pinot noirs, and with his inner eye he could see his cellars, the serried ranks of barrels, the heady fizz of fermentation, the bottles of Jensen wine on the glossy pages of the most prestigious publications. At that point, pinot noirs of finesse and quality were nowhere to be found in the New World. Worse (or better from Jensen's point of view), everybody who was anybody had concluded that the lively and capricious pinot noir just wouldn't adapt to the crude California sun, or would adapt only sullenly, grudgingly yielding up mediocre wines. Winemaker after winemaker had tried it, the making of great "burgundy," only to see the sun burn the fruit and the colour from the grape, and all the complexity, subtlety (and pure fun) just leached away. The heartbreak grape, indeed. The pragmatic professors at Davis declared the pinot noir unsuitable for California, and urged farmers to cut their losses and turn to something more tolerant of harsh conditions, like the cabernet sauvignon, the muscular and phlegmatic grape of Bordeaux, or the Syrah, the toast of the Rhône, or the zinfandel, native to who knows where, which was undergoing something of a renaissance at the time (or a fad, depending on your point of view).

"I thought I'd shoot the works on one big gamble," Jensen says now. "Can't grow pinot noir here, eh? No good in California and never will be, eh? I figured, as long as I'm gambling, I might as well not hedge my bets. Go for broke. Go for the big one. I planted all pinot noir."

Did anyone notice that he was ignoring their advice?

"No, only my family, my investors. They thought I was crazy too."

In the cellars of the Domaine de le Romanée-Conti, whenever Jensen poked about, asking questions, asking why they did this, didn't do that, shouldn't they be doing the other, he'd ask again and again: why are these wines so special? And they'd shrug, and say, ah, it's the soil, it's the limestone in the soil . . .

He wasn't the first American to run up against the French insistence on the primacy of soil as a determinant in the quality of wine. It was one reason the French were so slow to accept the possibility of superior California wines in the first place – they believed that nothing could replace the native genius of the soils of France. At Romanée-Conti they'd simply point to the limestone ridge behind them, where the crumbly rock had decomposed over the millennia and was being brought down by erosion to the deeper soils of the lower slopes. The crushed limestone, combined with the richer marl a third of the way up the slope, gives their wines their particular flavours. Not just at Romanée-Conti either. Whenever serious California winemakers prodded the French the response they'd get back invariably included the words "*climat*" and "*terroir*," the rough French equivalents of what some Americans were calling microclimate – some sort of fictive combination of moisture, soil, weather, slope, elevation and sunshine. But what the French really seemed to believe in, when push came to shove, was soil. This despite the unpublicized fact that Romanée-Conti itself constantly "improves" its soil with rich imported loam. (Perhaps the most celebrated soil improvement program in history was the 150 wagonloads of turf spread on its vineyards in the year 1749. The most notorious soil improvement, on the other hand, was the decision by the great champagne houses to import mulched and composted Parisian garbage to spread under the vines.)

Jensen came to share the French belief in soil. Nothing else seemed to account for the daily miracles he was tasting at the DRC.

"Remember, whenever I asked what it was that made their wines so special, they'd say, limestone soil. So . . . for me . . . limestone.

"People love to have theories about where quality comes from. For Francis Mahoney at Carneros, it's clones, the perfect vine. For others, it's the perfect barrel – say, three-quarters Tronçais and one-quarter Allier oak. Others think it's the perfect yeast, while others think it's the combination of malolactic and non-malolactic fermentations. Maybe it's all these things. For me, it came to be limestone."

His obsession with limestone was seen by the Keepers of the Recipe and the professors in California as an eccentricity that was likely to cause him rapid and well-deserved insolvency. They all believed – the New World believed – that climate was the key. Soil didn't matter. The sun did.

By European standards, most of California and Australia is too warm for good wine. In the early years, the Californians thought this an advantage; this extra heat would just guarantee a ripe crop every year. The professors at Davis, notably George Selleck's old friend Maynard Amerine, developed a Heat Summation Scale that categorized all regions in the state from One, the coolest, to Five, by measuring their average annual temperatures, and designated which grapes should be grown in each area. European theories about soil were thrown out the window. If the right grape was planted and European wine-making methods used or improved on, why then, by the use of superior technology the wines should taste even better.

And so they studied every minute aspect of the grape and its juice. They ran it through their laboratory analyses and their centrifuges and their spectraphotometers. They pulled out the malic, tartaric, citric, tannic and phosphoric acids, the proprionic and acetic acids; they made the malic over into lactic and studied that. They watched the long-chain polymers form in their Petrie dishes. They fermented at low temperatures and high, and then in the middle. They grew yeasts and mutated them. They killed off the wild yeasts, which is what they called native yeasts, and started again. They used glass and stainless steel and oak barrels. They pumped the wine over the cap instead of pushing it down. They filtered and fined, racked and drained. They did everything they could. And though they came up with some dull wines, "white-coat wines" as they were called, they also made some pretty interesting wines. What they didn't get, though, was an interesting pinot noir. The pinot noir continued to elude technological solution – the more sophisticated the technology, the more stubborn pinot noir became. The only thing they never seemed to learn was to leave pinot noir alone.

Jensen, as we shall see, didn't reject technology. But he wanted to use it as an aid to understanding, not as a substitute for it.

To believe that the centrifuge can help you make better pinot noir is like saying a computer can help a lover write better love letters. It can't. Only passion can do that.

All this really does set the professors' teeth on edge.

There's ample European evidence for the importance of *terroir*, crudely defined as soil, but in reality something closer to the *essence of place*, which includes the soil, the climate, the aspect, the slope, the way the soil is worked. Kermit Lynch, a romantic about wine and a fulminator against anything but the ancient methods, described in his book *Adventures on the Wine Route* how in some obscure hamlet north of Burgundy he came upon one of his suppliers. "He had three vineyards in three different *terroirs*, limestone, flint and clay, and he bottled them all separately. Here were wines from the same grape, the same cellar, vinification and vintage, but tasting them side by side one encountered three remarkably different personalities." Lynch's view is that the grape is dominant, but not a domestic tyrant; she must be part of a true *ménage a trois*, in love with both soil and climate.

In Josh Jensen's beloved Burgundy, they've no need for laboratory evidence or even for field trials to persuade them of the primacy of soil in this relationship. They had the evidence of their own senses and of hundreds of years of educated drinking planted deep in their psyches. André Noblet would simply pour a glass of his own Romanée-Conti and a glass of La Tâche, a contiguous parcel under the same proprietorship, and rest his case. The soils in those parcels are minutely different. In the labs, they've isolated a mineral in Meursault soil not found in the soil right next door at Puligny. The producers of those two great wines just *know* that the precise mineral composition of the soil is part of what they call the *goût de terroir*, the flavour of the place, and is the reason for the differences, minute but profound, between them.

It's possible for an educated palate, touring the small peasant proprietorships of Burgundy as well as the great *domaines*, to encounter pinot noirs that will taste and smell variously of cassis, cherry mint, blackberry, currant, raspberry, black cherry, and herbs of various kinds, and (if really educated) to place them precisely on the bench of the Côte d'Or.

The Burgundians will point out how accurate the ancient classifications of quality still are. Families come and go, they point out, winemaking changes and so do techniques. Fashions dictate changes in style. Why, even the climate changes. Only the *terroir* doesn't change, and the *terroir* dictates the character of the finished wine.

The Californians, for their part, point to the steadying influence of tradition as being at least as important as soil in this long continuity, since the Burgundians (they'll say, with some asperity) are not exactly experimenters at heart. But, the Burgundians reply, the New World cannot be expected to understand, since it's the trial and error of centuries that has established where each grape does best, right down to minute parcels of a particular field on a particular slope. It has worked for centuries. Why change?

The solution to the mystery very likely lies in Lynch's *ménage*, in some combination of factors – the composition of the soil and subsoil, its capacity to hold water and warmth matched against the water and warmth available, the vineyard's slope and elevation. Even then, a great crop will depend on the vigour of the vine, the care and tending it received, its pruning, and the number of sunlight hours it received at various stages in the season. From the time the vine buds to the vintage, every drop of rain, every hour of sunshine and degree of heat has its eventual effect on the finished wine. Too little rain in the spring is always a problem. Rain in September dilutes the grapes and creates the risk of mildew. The perfect balance between rain, sun, temperature and humidity has never been determined – the wine gets character from the interaction of them all. Bright sunlight ensures ripening, but overcast skies seem to enrich the grapes with minerals that give the wine long life and complexity.

For the purposes of our bottle of Calera Jensen pinot noir, it's enough to know that Josh Jensen's heart remained on the Côte d'Or. He'd sampled the Rhône, he'd done Bordeaux, he'd visited the Loire, and still Burgundy remained his obsession. "Pinot noir and chardonnay were exactly what I myself liked to drink, and I wanted to spend my life making things I'd want myself. This is a very subjective issue."

But he was the son of a dentist, not of a Baron, and he couldn't afford Burgundy itself.

In Burgundy, there was no longer mystery, only money. It was known exactly where good wine could be made, exactly where great wine could be made, and exactly where greater than great wine could be made. It was also known where those things were permitted to be done by bureaucratic fiat. And the prices of the real estate were exactly correlative to those qualities – to make great wine would cost, then, half a million dollars per acre. And now probably two million or more.

"And so with all the money I could scrape together from my family and everything and everyone I knew, I wouldn't have been able to get even an acre of green land in Burgundy, whereas the first property that I bought in San Benito County was 324 acres, and I got it for $18,000."

In any case, he wanted to go home to California to make his mark; he liked the challenge of trying to do well in a new place, the notion of being a pioneer, with its built-in unknowns and question marks.

The first thing he did when he returned to California was to visit the Bureau of Mines to obtain a set of geologic maps of the state. He was looking for limestone.

"The whole state has been meticulously mapped geologically. If you want, say, to find granodiorite rock, you can find it on the maps. If you want schist, basalt, whatever, you can find it on those maps. Unfortunately, it turns out the Golden State is pitifully thin in limestone." He looked everywhere, from the Oregon border to Los Angeles, but there was hardly any limestone to be found. There was much more in other states – Texas say, or Alabama – but he wanted to stay in California. "Partly because I was from here, and partly because it's a lot easier to do things when you have the structure of an industry near you. The Oregon industry didn't exist then, only a few pioneers starting up. And nothing very much in Texas."

He learned just enough geology to be able to tell one rock from another, and to be able to pick out what he wanted – the strata of calcareous (limestone-bearing) rock, or carbonine, a more general term that includes calcium carbonate (limestone itself). He'd also have settled for dolomite, which is half calcium carbonate and half magnesium carbonate.

Limestone doesn't always look like chalk, and it's easy to become confused. There is, however, a simple test, easy to perform – carbonate and dolomite will fizz in contact with hydrochloric acid.

"I had a Volkswagen camper when I came back from Europe, and I'd drive around to these places out in the boondocks. I'm surprised I didn't get shot. I'd drive to the end of these dirt roads, some of them pretty remote and obscure, spend the night, hike around the property, look at it from the road, and then, if it looked plausible, I'd find out if there was limestone there, as the map suggested.

"I had a small eyedropper and a tiny bottle of hydrochloric acid, and I'd dribble a few drops of acid onto the soil. In all that time, I never quite finished one bottle of acid. If it turned out the maps were right – they weren't always – and if the land was not too steep or too low or too high or too hot or too cold or too windy or too this or too that, I'd mark it down as promising. It couldn't be too close to a city, either. I didn't want to spend time and money and be enveloped in ten years by a mushrooming city. I didn't want to develop a world-class vineyard only to have it ripped out and turned into a supermarket.

"Oh, I looked everywhere. I looked at Trinity County,

practically at the Oregon border, up in some very high elevations. But it was too cold there, frost too late in the spring and into the summer. There are some nice limestone deposits in Big Sur, overlooking the ocean. But the climate on the Big Sur coast is wild – eighty-mile-an-hour winds, which would thrash the vines and defoliate them."

The land not only had to have limestone. It had to have a climate suitable for grape growing. "The Burgundians taught me that limestone made the best pinot noirs. Of course, you can grow pinot noir on other soils. And growing pinot noir on limestone in the middle of a desert is obviously not much use. Although . . ." – here he paused, and a thoughtful look came over his face – "it would be challenging to plant some pinot noir on limestone in tough conditions. A desert, though, would be maybe too tough. It's so hot that the grapes would have very little colour. Pinot noir tends to lose colour at high temperatures. So yes, the other factor was that once I had found some limestone I had to make sure it wasn't too hot, wasn't too cold, and in other ways was suitable."

He'd sift through the temperature and heat-gradient records kept by the state, but, with his inborn distrust of bureaucrats everywhere, also talked to the farmers surrounding the parcel he was interested in. "If they told me, yeah, I can grow peaches here, well, I knew I could also grow pinot noir grapes there."

To support himself while he was looking, he talked himself into a job as restaurant critic for the *San Francisco Chronicle*. "At that time, in 1972, there were no restaurant critics working in the city. They took a risk with me and I did it for two and a half years."

His family, his potential investors, were aghast at this

leisurely search for the perfect limestone vineyard. Other would-be winemakers bought a nice gentle slope somewhere, preferably in Napa or Sonoma (well, if you must have cool breezes for pinot noir why not around the southern end of Napa, in Carneros, close to the Bay?), and settled down right away to get on with it.

Josh didn't just want to make wine, though, he wanted to make the best pinot noir in America, and he was stubborn, so he persisted. He spent fully two years talking to suspicious cattlemen, grumpy landowners and hostile hunters. "Hello sir or ma'am, you don't know me but I'm just a young man looking for some property to buy, I want to plant a vineyard on your hillside, I'm going to grow one of the great wines of the world right here, yeah sure, you have some limestone on your property and that's why I'd like to buy this part of your land."

Yeah, right, they'd say, and chew a little tobacco, or spit a little, and then go back to their ranchhouses, shaking their heads.

He had to deal with the inborn conservatism of the ranchers, most of whom owned huge tracts of land and were hardly interested in severing small parcels of a hundred acres or so. "Even when I didn't get a flat-out no, they'd say, well, yeah, maybe, in some years perhaps, but they were never going to sell, not really."

After two years of searching, he came to the Gavilan Mountains. This was not, traditionally or obviously, grape country. There was one other winery, Chalone, on the other side of the mountains, facing the Salinas Valley and then the ocean. The eastern slopes were serious backcountry, less suitable for grapes than for manzanita and live oak, for cattle, for hunting, for wild boar and deer and game of all kinds, inaccessible and apparently hostile. Still, high up on Mt. Harlan, 2,000 feet above the sea, in virgin scrub, he squeezed his eyedropper and the acid danced and fizzed and sizzled . . . bingo!

A 324-acre parcel of Mt. Harlan was for sale. It was owned by a charitable foundation in San Francisco, a trust of the S.H. Powell Company, a mining operator. The founder, Henry Powell, had been the biggest limestone quarrier in the western U.S. at the turn of the century; he had owned limestone deposits all over the West, and made cement and other products. The company was left to his son, and his son left it to a charitable foundation. The property had last changed hands in 1903.

This $18,000 slice of paradise, a precipitous mountaintop made of limestone, containing the ruins of a limekiln and further ruins of a rock-crushing plant, had a few drawbacks, he admitted. First of all, he didn't have legal access – he'd have to cross someone else's land to get to his, something that offended his libertarian heart. Then, it had no water to speak of, only a creek that ran when it rained, which was when he didn't need a creek. Most of it was too steep to farm anyway, even for vineyards. The power company quoted him outrageous sums to run an electricity line to it, so he would have to do without power. How to pump the non-existent-as-yet water? He'd worry about that later. None of this mattered. It was affordable. He was only 27 years old, and he had a whole limestone mountaintop to himself.

The parcel he had to traverse to reach his own was, coincidentally, also 324 acres. It was owned by a widow, then aged 85.

Jensen asked her if she'd consider selling.

I don't wanna be a foolin' with it, I jus' don' wanna be a foolin' with it, she said, and dismissed him.

She looked in robust health, good for quite a few years. He didn't wish her ill. But he was as stubborn as she.

Every year, he'd take her flowers and chocolates on her birthday, and try to buy it from her, but she *jus' didn' wanna be a foolin' with it.*

He became quite fond of her. "You couldn't blame her for not selling," he says now, the grateful proprietor. "When people get old they're afraid they're going to get cheated, made a fool of, and it was just more trouble than it was worth to sell that thing as far as she was concerned."

She died in 1982 and her inheritor, her nephew, was happy to sell. For Jensen, it was a prudent buy. It cost him $150,000, much more than the $18,500 the first parcel cost, but it was well worth it. The second piece was contiguous to the first, and wrapped around it like a jigsaw piece. It gave him his legal access. It contained even more limestone than his original purchase and had a more secure water supply. It more than quadrupled his supply of plantable acres.

The original three vineyards, the Selleck, the Reed and the Jensen were all planted on the first parcel, and the newer Mills, chardonnay and viognier vineyards on the second. By 2006 his holdings were a good deal bigger – to the 648 acres of the first two pieces, and the 113 acres where his winery sits, he has added another 440 adjacent acres, a kind of land-bank reserve. Just over the hill from the winery building is a dolomite quarry, and Jensen's property overlooks it. He believes it would be "interesting" to attempt a wine from that soil, since it's analogous to limestone; and he went so far as to lay out vineyards before 9/11 put the project on hold. "In fact," he says, "there may be a spot, many spots, around here that would make even better wine than Calera does now. It's hard to believe I picked the perfect spots first try. And here's another challenge: there may be places in other states where there's limestone, where we could make good pinots – Texas, say, or Alabama."

Mt. Harlan, however, gave him what he wanted. The heavy limestone deposits crowning the peak ensured that the easily erodable rock travelled downhill, washing into the soil.

Better, it was only 35 miles from the Pacific and Monterey Bay, and the fog funnelled in by coastal valleys all summer creates warm days and cool nights – ideal conditions for pinot noir. The determinant of the climate in California is always the ocean – the closer to the ocean, the cooler the vineyards are. This is true even in the Napa valley, where the coolest area is down along the San Pablo Bay, San Francisco Bay and Carneros. Jensen usually harvests a full two weeks after Carneros and Sonoma. "The climate is great, not like Burgundy. I've always thought that great wines are produced in Burgundy despite their crappy weather, not because of it. A friend of mine lived in Dijon for exactly a year and says he saw the sun only nine days. Here, we do get fog and the benefits of the marine influence, but we don't get that horrible icy wind that the Salinas Valley gets off Monterey Bay. In fact, the way we keep our winery cool is by fans that come on at night and blow in the cool night air.

"So limestone isn't enough by itself. If that was all there was, you could mix it into your soil and plant wherever you wanted. Mt. Harlan gave me the other ingredients too. Still, in my opinion, climate is secondary to soil."

It's one thing to own a mountain of scrub and limestone and

have the intention to make a wine to rival the great wines of Vosne-Romanée, but how do you get *there* from *here*?

For all the years of his search, Jensen had been keeping mental lists, picking up skills where he could. It was easy to see what was needed. He could tick them off in his head. You need somewhere to live. You need machinery – you're a farmer now. You need to be able to rip out the manzanita and scrub oaks, root and branch, but mostly root, so you need a deep cultivator. You need a tractor to prepare the land. You need mechanical hoes and mowers. You need power in the fields, a generator. You need fences, miles of fencing and thousands of posts, to keep out the deer and the boar. Gates and locks. You need trellis posts and trellis wire, figure the rows about 10 feet apart, that's about a mile an acre, figure 24 miles of trellis to start. You need water. Your creek runs dry in the critical months, so you need shallow (you hope) wells to start. You need pumps. You need an irrigation system. Drip irrigation along every row to every vine. Another 24 miles, of hose this time.

And of course you need vines. What rootstock and what clone to graft? Where do you get 'em? How to be sure of quality?

That's just the vineyard.

You want to make wine in the meantime? To buy grapes from somewhere else for a year or so while your vines mature? You need a winery. Can be just a shed, a warehouse, but then you'll need labour, and pumps and . . . what else?

For starters, you'll need crushers and de-stemmers and fermentation tanks, preferably stainless steel and expensive. Another mile or so of food-grade plastic hose. Presses. Storage tanks. Settling and mixing tanks. Barrels – you want to make good wine, you have to buy oak barrels, preferably from France.

You can't handle and clean all those yourself – you must have hired hands. You need somewhere to fine the finished wines. You need a bottling plant . . . Well, maybe the bottling plant can wait until your wine is readier. Scrap the bottling plant for now. Check into mobile plants like they have elsewhere. Look into bottles, corks. Have to have labels, too – better think about a design. And a name. You'll need an inventory control system of some kind . . .

You'll need all of these things before you can make wine. And then you'll have to keep the wine for a year or two before it's ready to sell, so you need warehouse space. And time.

Most of all, what you need is money. Lots and lots of money.

CHAPTER SIX

*In which hilltop wilderness is
turned into vineyards and given
suitable names. The first vines are
acquired and planted*

The first 324 acres cost Jensen $18,500, and he put that up himself. Then he went looking for money. The first source was family.

"My dad encouraged me to start the winery, and invested in the project in the beginning when, I must say with 20-20 hindsight, it certainly had to look like a harebrained scheme." He remained Josh's partner until he died in 1996. And so Jensen Jr. formed a partnership with his family – his parents, actually, since brother and sister sensibly declined – and Bill Reed (the only non-family member he's ever taken on as a partner, except for the silent and brooding presence of various banks). Father and mother were, at first, amused by their son's growing obsession, for obsession it was, as Josh now willingly admits. "They were amused and interested at first, and subsequently they were sort of horrified," he says, cheerfully unmoved by any trauma he might have inflicted on them.

Bill (William Garrard) Reed, the Reed of the eponymous Calera vineyard named after him, did have some connection, however distant, with family, and Josh always felt they were "almost related." Reed was born in Shelton, Washington, in 1908, and died in Seattle in 1989. His grandfather, Sol Simpson, had been employed by Jensen's mother's family in the northwest lumber business before starting his own small operation, Simpson Timber Company, on a hope and a prayer. His son-in-law, Mark Reed, built the company into a strong regional presence, and then Bill, in a spectacular business career that started in 1931, lifted Simpson into the ranks of major American companies. Josh remembers him with great affection. "In 1971 he graciously stepped aside as CEO, even though he really had no desire to retire, when his own son, William Jr., said he was ready to run the company. How many fathers would do that?"

For years Reed Sr. wrote the brash young winemaker a stream of unfailingly encouraging letters, always supportive and upbeat, even during the long years when Calera was clearly struggling and a number-crunching capitalist would have recommended liquidation. Josh believes that Reed's decision to invest in Calera at the outset was crucial, because it appeared to validate the project, particularly with the banks. "He even put up with having to go down to the Seattle police station to get fingerprinted, part of the glamour of owning a winery, courtesy of the bureaucrats."

In 1981 Josh wanted to increase his personal ownership of Calera, and asked Reed if he'd sell his interest. The old man was reluctant because he enjoyed the eccentric investment, but agreed. "We had the shortest, easiest negotiation I'd had in my business career. Bill sold me his interest, and remained a true friend and Calera booster always."

To buy Reed's share, to inject more money into a cash-starved operation, and also to have a little something for himself (he was by then raising a family, having married Jeanne a few years earlier) Josh needed a source of cash. His mother's family still controlled a small privately owned lumber company, the primary source of her family's wealth. Josh had inherited a small block of stock in the company, and wanted to sell it.

This wasn't so easy. A tiny interest in a privately held lumber company in the Northwest? How to value it? How to introduce non-family investors to a family business? "My uncles . . . Well, they didn't want to help me in my folly. They kept saying they didn't want me to make a fool of myself. That was understandable. Nor was it a minority opinion at the time. I remember many people telling me I was a fool, that I was going to lose my shirt. I said, unless I sell my stock I won't even have a shirt to lose. Of course, after it became clear I was going to make it, behind my back the same people would say, Oh, anybody could have done that, it was so predictable, it was like shooting fish in a barrel. Though, to give them credit, there were also people who told me I was going to lose my ass, and told my family that, and some of them are the people who now come up to me and tell me, you remember what I told you? How wrong I was!"

His uncles delayed and stalled, always ready with a good reason not to give him money. "Maybe it was the taxes . . . Then it was, No, we'd like to buy you out but even if we wanted to we couldn't because there's this paragraph, or this subsection, there's something else . . . They always found reasons why not, never a reason for. It was all baloney. So I set out on a four-year project to try to sell my stock. Eventually I sold it."

His partners – his father and Bill Reed, mostly – were co-owners of the winery only, not the vineyards. "In the Burgundy model," Josh says, "which is also my model, the vineyards are everything, the winery nothing. A winery is just a place to store barrels." In this unique case, this is not entirely true: the Calera winery, gaunt and ugly as it is, or rather was, is more than a warehouse. It's still one of the few (perhaps the only) entirely gravity-operated wineries in the world, and valuable for that. Nevertheless, his heart is up in the hills, where the grapes are, and he owned the vineyards outright until he started giving parcels to his kids, late in the 1990s. It's the land and the vines he feels most fiercely protective about. All else is replaceable.

"The first thing I did after I bought the land was fence it. I had to, or the deer would have gotten everything. Then I planted my test crops, and began to farm. I sort of picked up all the necessary skills along the way, by asking questions and watching."

He was living in a trailer with his wife and two small children.

"Remember, when I bought the place, up where the vine-yards are, there was no electricity, no telephone, no paved roads, no anything. It was back in the boondocks. There was water, but no pumps. No civilization at all, so I rented a five-acre piece from a rancher at the bottom of the hill, where there was a paved road, electricity and a telephone. The trailer was 12 feet by 50 feet, a mobile home, and *small* . . ." The young family lived in it for four and a quarter years before starting to build a house in 1978.

Josh acquired the first vineyard parcel in 1974, and planted the first three vineyards, the Jensen, the Reed and the Selleck, the following year. Three years after that, in 1977, he bought the parcel that now contains the winery, closer to Hollister, the nearest town, along the Cienaga Road. At 113 acres, it might seem overlarge for a winery, but in ranch country 100 acres was a small parcel, as small as anyone would sever. The second vineyard parcel, where the Mills, the chardonnay and the viognier vineyards are now planted, came in 1982.

"It takes about 20 minutes to drive from Hollister to our winery, and about 30 minutes from the winery up to the vineyards. It's quite steep, another 1,000 feet up. The Gavilan hills start in San Juan Bautista and peter out around King City, so ours is a relatively small mountain. But it's ours, our own mountain."

On March 2, 1974, Josh Jensen took a tractor up the mountainside, ripped out the brush from a small parcel, and with as many friends as he could round up he planted 500 test vines of pinot noir. He remembers the date so precisely because he had only closed escrow on the property the previous day. "I had the rootings already there from the nursery, and if something had snagged the closing of that escrow it would have been big trouble.

"That test patch of 500 was just to see if they'd be killed by some killer fungus that nobody had ever heard of before. Or, if it would turn out that it was always minus 30 degrees in the winter but nobody had ever realized it because nobody had ever lived up there. Or maybe there was some secret bug or virus or nematode or some other climatic catastrophe that would render it unsuitable.

"Anyway, they seemed to grow okay, although I couldn't give them enough water – just hand watering from a little jury-rigged tank on the back of a pickup. So in 1975 we put in the rest of what were to be the original 24 acres, and put in the real irrigation system, an aboveground drip system."

Those 500 vines were to become part of the Jensen vineyard, named after his father. They are now 31 years old, or "in 30th leaf." The rest of the Jensen's 13,000 or so vines were planted the following year. They are in 29th leaf. They are where our bottle of wine grew under the California sun.

The summer of 1974 Josh Jensen rode the tractor every day, taking his lunch in the fields, coming home to his trailer sweaty and happy. First the hillsides were plotted and laid out, and the three individual vineyards were laid out. The vineyard boundaries are entirely arbitrary – or at least unrelated to soil analysis or other careful matters – which makes the difference in their wines so interesting. The terrain was so rough there was no choice but to plant a little bit here and a little bit over yonder. It would have been cheaper and far easier to farm on an ongoing basis if he'd been able to plant one continuous carpet of vineyard. Alas, such was not the case. The boundaries were determined in a simple way: Jensen would start the tractor at the creek and work his way uphill until it starting slipping, which marked the boundary of that parcel. The process was repeated on the other side of the creek, which yielded another five acres before the tractor couldn't get any higher.

Then the designated slopes were brushed and the trees stumped. The slash was carted away and burned. The hillside was combed by a giant tractor with three deep shanks three feet apart and as deep as six feet down, first one way across the vineyards, and then a second pass at right angles. This was not to break up any hardpan, for Calera had none. What it did was to break up the soil to allow deep penetration by the vine roots, and to comb out any remaining tree roots. It was tricky work – the tractor would pull deep ripping shanks straight up some pretty steep slopes, difficult even for a very large machine, but Josh remembers the work fondly. "I was clearing the trees and the brush and getting it burned and fenced, and for me those are some of my happiest memories, those days when I'd work for three days in a row without talking to anybody, because I'd be living in my camper up in the vineyard, on my mountaintop. I'd be up driving the tractor at seven in the morning, and I'd take things like hardboiled eggs into the fields. I was never trained to drive a tractor, do construction work. I just picked it up as I went along. I don't drive tractors any more, and I miss it. It was very satisfying to do a good job at that."

By the spring of 1975 he had three vineyards. Since his training and inclination were Burgundian, it was natural to harvest each plot separately and treat that batch of grapes as a separate wine, in the Burgundian fashion. He'd seen how identifiably distinct were the pinot noirs made from contiguous parcels in Burgundy, and he was sure the same would happen at Calera. It remained only to come up with a name for each parcel and its wine.

In Burgundy the nomenclature had evolved over centuries. There were village names and commune names and names for individual fields. There were fanciful names such as Bâtard-Montrachet and Les Amoureuses, all of them mossy with age, venerable with tradition and inflexible by bureaucratic edict. Jensen thought briefly about such descriptive site names as Centre Canyon or South Slope, but they seemed banal. Stag's Leap was taken and Boar's Run or Gopher Field didn't seem to lend the right tone. In the end he decided to honour some of the men who had helped and inspired him to start and nurture Calera by naming a vineyard after each.

The first and primary vineyard, and at just under 14 acres the second largest, is named for his father Stephen. The second, its 4.4 acres at sometimes alarming angles, is called Reed, after his first partner, Bill Reed. The third, a 4.8-acre parcel, was named for George Selleck, who had introduced him to wine in the first place. The fourth and until recently the final parcel, added in 1982, is the 14.4-acre Mills vineyard, named for John Everett Mills.

Mills was born in San Francisco in 1912, and died in Hollister in 1985. Jensen met him in the early 1970s when he was still searching for limestone. "I confided that I probably had more money than sense and he instantly replied, 'Great! That's what we need out here!'" Mills's family had moved to the Hollister area shortly after he was born. His mother died when he was 13, his father five years later, so at age 18 he found himself sole support of three younger sisters and a younger brother. He managed somehow. He did hard physical work all his life. At various times he worked in the wheatfields of Canada, in mines in Mexico, at Permanente Cement, and at the old W.A. Taylor Winery on Cienaga Road, about a mile north of where Calera is now located. For much of his later life he worked for Archie Hamilton, an eccentric mining entrepreneur. In the 1950s Everett built a series of terraces and retaining walls at Hamilton's Cienaga Road property, as the start of a hillside rock-crushing plant, but Hamilton soon changed his mind, abandoning the walls and terraces to the elements and the weeds. That, of course, became the Calera winery. As Jensen later wrote, in one of his mailers, "It was more than 20 years later, in 1977, that an eccentric wine guy named Jensen bought the property with the crazy idea of using those same terraces to make the world's first and only completely gravity-flow winery."

After abandoning the Cienaga Road site, Hamilton and Everett built an even more elaborate structure up on his mountaintop limestone deposit, near the top of the Gavilan Mountains. Then Hamilton died suddenly, and it too was abandoned. "I started trying to buy that property in 1972 from Hamilton's widow," Josh recalls, "and that was how I came to meet Everett, who by that time was more or less retired but was still keeping an eye on things for Mrs. Hamilton. When we were building the winery, Everett would stop by from time to time to keep an eye on us and make sure these city slickers didn't do too many stupid things. In his latter years I guess you could say Everett worked for me.

"He used cusswords prodigiously, in fact, practically as much as I do. I delivered the eulogy at his funeral."

The last of the named parcels is the 13.1-acre Ryan vineyard, planted in 1998 and 2001. It was named for Jim Ryan, the vineyard manager, the naming coming as a complete surprise to Ryan himself, who had never expected such an honour – the naming ceremony was held at the vineyard, and Ryan's far-flung family came to Calera to acknowledge the occasion, the kids getting time off school for the purpose. If you ask him about it now, he just splutters and looks sheepish, but he was moved by the gesture and no one would mind if he paid just a little bit more attention to the vines there than to the others.

The soil in all five vineyards, as well as in the unnamed Zones, contains the requisite limestone, but is otherwise generally poor, thin in nutrients, granular in texture, its problems compounded by two long droughts in the 30 years of cultivation. It's deep in places – in spots they've dug down five or eight feet and still found soil – but it's not very fertile. "There's an old saying in Burgundy," Jensen says with philosophical optimism, "that asserts that if the soil in Burgundy weren't the richest in the world it would be the poorest, by which they mean that if you grew potatoes or carrots there, you wouldn't get very many potatoes or carrots. Like Burgundy, our land is worth a million or it's worth nothing."

Still, at his prodding and under Ryan's direction, cultivation techniques have been changed to enrich the soil. Large amounts of compost are added each year, fallow crops are sown between rows (peas, often – it's one of the rare cover crops that tastes good). Ryan used to spray chemical herbicides under the vines, but has abandoned the practice, and now hoes by hand. As a consequence, the soil has greatly improved and crop yields have increased.

As Jensen's Burgundian perspective would suggest, the soil in each parcel contains minute differences, not just in its upper few feet, but for the 30 or 40 feet that the vine roots reach.

The Selleck has a lot of decomposed granite, and there are limestone outcroppings above the vineyard – just like the Côte d'Or. The limestone at the top has eroded and washed downhill, and it has its influence on the soil – Selleck contains more limestone than the others. Its soil is also more granular and lighter in colour – brown with a little bit of red. The Reed vineyard has the deepest, darkest soils. Before it was cleared, the Reed slope was a mixed oak and pine forest with a lot of leaf mould, and its soil is blacker, with more clay. Its exposure is northerly, and the sun leaves it earlier in the day, so it's always the last of the three vineyards to ripen. The Mills is the lowest in elevation. The Ryan is a lighter, more textured soil, and is the highest of all the vineyards, a good 500 feet above the others.

Within each vineyard there are markedly different exposures along the mountain's irregular flank. The Jensen, for instance, is usually harvested over the course of a full month, because its south-facing vines mature much more rapidly than its north-facing ones.

Although he has no intentions of doing so, Josh believes he could make at least eight markedly different pinot noirs from the current vineyards.

In 2006, the Jensen vineyard still had one niggling problem – the bottom few rows of the vineyard always seemed to produce wines that were thin and watery. Jensen even budded over two rows to Aligoté, a varietal that crops heavily and is more forgiving of poor soils. It was only in 2005 that the light suddenly went on – the vines were watery because . . . because, hey, they were getting too much water . . . The drip irrigation system, as the pressure builds up, waters the lowest few rows first. Then, when it is turned off, the water slowly pools at the bottom of the hill. As a result, the last few rows were getting triple doses of water. In 2005 Ryan shut off the irrigation to those rows first – problem solved.

The as-yet unnamed vineyard, divided for convenience only into Red, Green and Yellow Zones, was still giving trouble in 2006, and the winery was wrestling with how to solve the problem. I sat in on a tasting in the lab in February, and confirmed the lamentable fact that the wines the vineyard was producing were too tannic. The vineyard is sited between the Jensen and the Mills, and Jensen had hoped optimistically to add sections of it to those named parcels instead of creating an entirely new one. It didn't look as though that was going to happen any time soon.

Diana Vita's view, after the tasting, was that they'd have to give the vineyard its own name after all, and manage the wines accordingly. Jensen wanted to try another experiment first, picking across rows instead of with them. "The big part of the new field goes over the hilltop," he pointed out. "But we simply follow the rows when we pick. As a result, this year we were picking at 26 per cent sugar in the yellow zone and only 21 in the red. If we picked instead from west to east, we may correct the problem. Let's try that in 2006."

In 1978 he made 700 cases of pinot noir from the young vines in his own vineyards, all in half bottles. It was small, a very modest production. But it was his own, his first vintage. He put a few bottles aside, to build the winery's "library," or archive. Maybe one day he'd give a bottle to Madame Lalou ...

CHAPTER SEVEN

*In which clones are seen to
be important. So is the TLC
given the vines and the way
they are managed*

 You don't just phone up a nursery and say, *Send me over 15,000 young pinot noir plants.* Not if you're driven by that entrepreneurial single-mindedness that teeters between insistence and obsession. Not if you want to prove the nay-sayers wrong, the doubters and scoffers, not if you *know* it can be done if you have the right place and the right methods and the right . . . raw materials.

To make great wine you also need healthy, vigorous vines. And for the correct vines you need to select the right clone.

Remember that pinot noir had, at last count, more than 200, or 500, or 1,000, clonal variations, ranging from the heavy-cropping *pinot droit* to the small-berried, tiny-bearing *pinot fin*, the vine of Romanée-Conti, and that it mutates, fades and reconstitutes itself more capriciously than any other of the vinifera varieties; remember that pinot noir is one of thousands of varieties of *Vitis vinifera*, all of which are tragically susceptible to the phylloxera louse, and for safety sake must be grafted to American rootstocks to protect it from infection (does the graft interpose a barrier to the free rising of sap? No one knows for sure); remember that there are shy-bearing and prolific clones, upright and spreading clones, large-berried clones and small; remember all this and . . . how do you choose?

A clone is a population of plants all of which are the descendants of a single individual and are, therefore, genetically identical. Clones have historically been arrived at through mutation and selection. This is not exactly new – the first clones were propagated well before Roman times, when some neolithic farmer hit on the radical notion of propagating through cuttings instead of cross-fertilization, thereby arriving at the modern vineyard, which consists entirely of sexless – or hermaphrodite – plants.

By historical accident clonal selection in California was left largely to vine growers and viticulturalists (that is, farmers) and not to winemakers, and has therefore been driven more by the need to improve yields and resist diseases than by a search for anything as elusive as quality. This wouldn't have harmed the industry – after all, disease-free vines benefit everyone – if the winemakers had done their part. But they didn't. In the 1970s and 1980s the winemakers came to rely on technological solutions to enological problems. *You have poor grapes and you want fine wines? No problem! Extract the maximum colour and tannin by extended maceration! Centrifuge the sucker! Fire it up with off-the-shelf superyeasts!*

"I'm not a clone man," Josh Jensen says. "I believe in the primacy of soil. However, having said that, it's important to have a proper clone. It's important that your pinot noir vines are small-clustered, small-berried and low yielding. It's important that you have the real thing and not some mutant, light-skinned, overproducing Gamay Beaujolais or something similar."

But . . . a vine can take seven years to reach full-bearing maturity. It can take *years* – up to 15 years in one notorious case, Jensen's own viognier – for approved imported stock to clear quarantine regulations and actually reach the grower. And humans fade faster than vines do – the average winemaker has only about 30 or 40 chances in his lifetime to attempt to make superlative wines. You don't want some grim mutant growing in your vineyard to spoil half a dozen of those chances. You want the right stuff, right off.

Which is why everyone cheerfully believes the rumours that Jensen's pinot noir stock came directly from the Domaine de la Romanée-Conti itself, bypassing Customs, quarantine and the prying eyes of bureaucratic inspectors. Or, if not directly, via Chalone. Or possibly that Chalone got its cuttings from Jensen, who got them, somehow, from the DRC, probably by visiting the place and stuffing his raincoat pockets full of vineyard cuttings, which he propagated on a patch of Chalone vineyard when he got to California. Of course, this could just be a canard made up to spook the bureaucrats, who are (rightly) worried about the importation of noxious pests. Bureaucrats just don't understand the passion – the obsession, the Burgundy obsession – for quality.

Whatever the reality, Jensen's "suitcase clones" have become legend in California, and have subsequently mutated into the "Calera clone" in the minds of the state's high-end pinot growers. A piece in 2003 by Rod Smith in the *Los Angeles*

Times, on the "cult winery" called Flowers Estate, is typical. Smith uses a few paragraphs discussing the "sexy Dijon clones" that became available to American winemakers in the 1990s, which were rejected by the Flowers' winemaker, Hugh Chappelle, in favour of the Calera clone. "The so-called Calera clone actually has a dozen or more variations," Smith wrote. "They all originated with the single unregulated or suitcase clone that reportedly was taken from one of Burgundy's greatest vineyards more than 20 years ago. Since then it has been distributed and repropagated throughout California, developing different characteristics in different sites." Chappelle told the writer he had no fewer than 11 variations of the Calera clone in his vineyards. "We just know that Calera gives very complex and interesting wines here," he said. And Smith adds: "More than the Swan or Dijon clone wines, the Caleras were mysteriously evocative, shaded and nuanced."

In 2006 Jensen was still getting calls from other winemakers looking for cuttings from his vines, including a call from Gallo of Sonoma. It is not a big business, though, at $1 a cutting, but he seldom refuses.

I offered to turn my tape recorder off while we discussed this matter of clonal origin. Jensen thought this was a good idea, and I did so. In a while, I turned it back on.

"Whether or not our clone comes from Romanée-Conti . . . ," he was saying, "that in itself wouldn't mean the wines will taste like Romanée-Conti wines. It would just mean that you've got a true, well-selected pinot noir stock and not a mutant, and that you'd be starting with a good chance instead of with two strikes against you."

So it's fair to say that all of the Selleck, all of the Reed and about two-thirds of the Jensen vineyards are planted with this Romanée-Conti-rumoured clone. Unless of course they came from somewhere else, from Chalone maybe, or just from bench grafts from a nursery in St. Helena, California – off-the-shelf pinot noir, as is the remainder of the Jensen.

He did buy some vines from St. Helena. Every year, while he searched for the perfect vineyard, he put in an order. "To really be sure of getting the stuff you have to order a year in advance. Then I'd cancel at the last moment, because I hadn't found my land yet and so had nowhere to plant them, and reorder again for the next year." Finally, having acquired the land, he bought 15,000 plants, at $1 a plant and 25 cents for the grafting rootstock. "We got them planted, me and my friends, that first year. We planted the rootstock, the business part of the vine, a thing about six or nine inches long. This has a few buds on the top and some rootlets on the bottom. You graft the buds onto the top once it's in the ground, after the first year. We did that in 1975. A cutting from the desired plant, the scion, cigar thick, is cut into the rooting with a single dovetail."

All Calera's pinot noir vines are grafted onto nursery-bought rootstock, with the exception of the largest vineyard, the Mills, which is still "own-rooted" – not grafted at all – as are the Mt. Harlan chardonnay and the second and largest of the viognier plantings. The Mills, chardonnay and some viognier, therefore, are pure vinifera to the ends of their rootlets, which in turn means they are completely vulnerable to the phylloxera louse – 100 per cent vulnerable and, once infected, 100 per cent dead. This is high-risk farming. Why does he take the risk?

Phylloxera vastatrix, the louse that nearly destroyed the European wine industry in the 19th century, was first seen in

Europe in 1869, and it exploded through the wine-growing world with a ferocity and vigour that left no defence. The louse had originally come from North America, whose vines had coexisted with it for millennia and had therefore developed an immunity; the nick-of-time solution was to graft the chosen clonal cutting onto a root of American origin.

Now phylloxera is back in California. There is some controversy about this. The scientists at Davis are calling it Phylloxera Type B, and say it's a new and more virulent mutant. Jensen feels that this talk of mutants is an attempt to fudge their own ambivalent role in recent clonal propagation.

"They haven't been reading their mail," he says. "The French have been warning for years that the hybrid rootstocks they've been pushing on everyone are not safe, are not sufficiently resistant. But it was high yielding stock, and winemakers planted it on their say-so and because others were doing so. Well, the French were right. Many people planted vines on these hybrids, one was called ARGI, and, I think the clone number on another was 1202, and now they're being hit. And once the louse is in your vineyard, it's over. One vine this year, 30 acres the next, 300 the year after that ..." There are hundreds of planters in Napa who are faced with the ruinous cost of replacing all their vines. Almost 80 per cent of Napa and Sonoma are vulnerable.

So is Calera's Mills vineyard, but Jensen greets the suggestion with the same philosophical shrug with which he responds to questions about the San Andreas Fault. "Our vineyards are extremely isolated, 100 miles south of San Francisco, and there are no vineyards nearby. The closest one is a mile away but 2,000 feet below us in elevation. Hopefully, if there's any serious spread of phylloxera or Pierce's or anything like that it would take a very long time for the organisms to get up the mountain to our vineyard."

He is, however, being careful. Vehicles that have visited Napa wineries are strongly discouraged from the Calera vineyards, and visitors are taken up in the winery's truck or in Jensen's van, with its Mr. Pinot licence plate.

Calera's vineyards, even without phylloxera or Pierce's, took a long time to come up to full bearing. Back-to-back droughts, rabbits, birds, gophers, deer, wild pigs, ground squirrels, mildew, leaf roll virus, oak root fungus, leaf hoppers and thrips – all took their toll. So have downy mildew, oidium or "powdery mildew," white, black and grey rot, red spiders, grubs of the cochylis and eudemis moths, various sorts of beetles, mites and grubs of all kinds. (Most of these are easily combatted by the so-called Bordeaux mixture spray, a mix of copper sulphate and lime, which leaves the vines a garish blue until it washes off, but has the twin virtues of being biodegradable and environmentally benign.) Leaf roll virus is Calera's biggest problem. It doesn't kill the vine, but weakens it and damages the berries.

If, as Josh Jensen believes, it's the vineyard (defined as soil and subsoil, slope, water and drainage, temperatures and sunlight) that imparts character to the wine, if the wine you drink is somehow an expression of the fruit you pick, then the choices made in the vineyard are crucial to the quality of the wine itself. A minimalist approach will only take a winemaker so far. Jensen's friend Jacques Seysses, of the Domaine Dujac in Morey-St.-Denis, Burgundy, may believe that because his vineyards are perfectly sited to grow perfect grapes his job is merely to let nature take its course and "make wine the lazy way." But the vineyard will only impart character, and mediocre wines can have great character. The winemaker's job is to control for quality. If the grapes are the horse, the winemaker must act as the jockey.

California winemakers went through their period of trying to make silken wines from sour grapes. The technocratic manipulation of the wine in the winery eventually ran its course and, led by people like Josh Jensen, there's been a return to low-tech, careful winemaking. An aspect of this more humble attitude is an acknowledgment that the raw material is crucial. Great wine, as the Europeans have been saying for centuries, is grown in the vineyard.

The vineyard, therefore, is where the next great increases in quality are to be found, the next incremental improvements.

A great crop depends on the health and aggressiveness of the vine, the babysitting it receives, the way it's pruned, and the amount of sun it receives at various stages in the season. Grapes will reflect every drop of moisture, every ray of sunlight, every degree of warmth. As Jensen puts it, "From here, smart farm managers, soils guys, can help us greatly."

Some of the vineyard choices are: where to plant, what rootstocks to plant, what clones to graft, what weight of crop (yield) to demand, how to lay out the vineyard (how far apart the rows, how far apart the vines?), how to trellis, what pruning technique to use, sunlight, how to manage water (the thorny question of irrigation). And then the questions of sprays, fertilizers, pests and diseases, thinning and selection of the crop, and when to pick.

After that, it's over to the winery.

For the purposes of our bottle, we have the Jensen vineyard, almost 14 acres of crumbly limestone soil, sloping in four directions at once. Some of its vines are planted with store-bought pinot noir; much of the rest may or may not come from the Domaine de la Romanée-Conti, but its vines resemble very closely those of that eminent *domaine* – producing small bunches with very small berries, yielding a high skin-to-juice ratio. They are growing on a rootstock called St. George.

Those are the givens.

The Jensen pinot noirs are planted in rows ten feet apart, wide enough for tractors and other equipment to move comfortably, and the plants themselves are six feet apart; there are 726 vines per acre. The newer vineyards are planted to a different pattern, the rows seven and a half or eight feet apart, the vines spaced at four and a half or five feet, giving a greater density per acre, around 1,278 in the case of the Ryan. The winery has had to buy smaller tractors to fit between the narrower rows.

Pinot noir vineyards look different wherever they are. On the chilly, chalky soil of sun-starved Champagne, they look maniacally regular. In Burgundy, moist and fecund but shy of sun, the rows are close, the bushes dense and close-cropped. In Australia, where sun is a friend and a threat, the rows are wild and impenetrable. In foggy, windy Carneros, they huddle close. Up in the mountains along the Cienaga Road, water is the critical resource, and the vines, while each is rumpled and untidy, are spaced at intervals so that the roots do not fight for each drop of moisture. The Jensen vineyard's 726 per acre is less than half the European norm.

Until the last few years, all Calera's vines were pruned and trained to a modified cordon system on a three-wire trellis. At the end of each annual cycle, when the grapes have been picked and the vines have gone dormant, they were cut back to two three-foot-long "cordons," which are trained horizontally along the lowest of the three wires. A selected number of buds, usually 12, were left on each cordon. In the spring the shoots were trained upwards and tied to the two upper wires, giving the right balance of leaf to fruit.

There are many other methods of pruning: the espalier and "goblet" systems are the most common. Others are cane-pruning, fan-pruning, low-bush training, and high trellising, with many variations on each. Starting in 2003, Ryan began converting some of the vines to a cane-pruning style, the new canes arching out of the trunk itself, with no cordons. It remains to be seen what affect this has on yield, but Ryan believes that with the newly more-fecund soil, yields should start to climb.

Josh Jensen generally defers to Ryan on pruning matters. "It's always been the area of the business that I know the least about. In the early years I was the vineyard manager, and it's one reason why the vines got off to a bad start."

The idea behind pruning, which is essentially a kind of "vegetable editing" in Hugh Johnson's phrase, is to control yield – either to maximize yield and ripeness, as in Germany, or in more torrid climates like Spain, to restrict them. The more arid the area, the wider apart the vines and the more floppy the canopy of foliage to protect the berries from the sun. In wetter regions you plant close to prevent each vine being drowned with too much water.

In the Jensen vineyard "canopy management" is an ongoing experiment. This means picking selected leaves off in the growing season from the canes and around the berry clusters. Calera believes it improves the wine. "I think it accelerates ripening, gives better acid, lowers pH and cuts down on mildew. It also increases the phenolics – the complexity of flavour and the volatile aromas. It adds colour too."

It also has another advantage. At the base of each leaf is a bud, and the amount of sun each bud receives governs whether it becomes leaf or fruit the following year. Selected leaf thinning can thus have a considerable effect on the crop the following year. A heavy canopy of leaves will make the vine throw out more foliage, and less fruit. Hence the trellising method pulls the fruiting canes upwards, which pulls the leaves away from the fruit, exposing the berries to the sun.

In parts of France, particularly Bordeaux, pruning is entrusted only to experienced people intimate with the vineyard, the vine and the *terroir*. In Australia, where they haven't quite gotten over their technophilia, they are experimenting with a pruning method that more nearly resembles hedgerow management – simply cutting everything with circular saws into a neat hedge. They claim it works just as well. At Calera all pruning is done by hand by the vineyard crew and whatever hired help is available. It can take several months to complete.

The first problem a winemaker faces, after planting and vineyard layout, is the thorny question of yield. In France, it's axiomatic that low yields intensify flavours. A smaller crop gives you a darker, richer berry that's more flavourful and intense; the bunches sit apart on the vine and they don't rot as easily. The fruit can be left on the vine longer without risk, and the grapes mature better. Of course, in Burgundy, which is at the northern end of acceptability for red grapes, low yields have another advantage, which has surely coloured its codification of low yields into ironclad edicts (high yields automatically "declassify" the wine from that vintage, degrading a Vosne-Romanée, for instance, to a mere bourgogne): a small crop will also ripen faster.

Bearing a heavy crop is as stressful to a vine as childbirth is to a woman. But what is "heavy"? What is "high yield"? In California, with its abundant sunshine, bigger crops can ripen well, and the Burgundian axiom might be false. Still, it's fair to say that most quality producers believe in low yields.

It's also fair to say that grape growers don't.

Nor, indeed, do the winemakers' bankers, who regard yield as just another name for productivity, and bankers *love* productivity, because it improves the cash flow (in the short term) and pays down those inevitable loans more quickly.

(For the same reason, those few bankers who know wine are suspicious of pinot noir – fickleness is not a bankerly approved quality. They don't like its changeableness, nor the time it takes to store it before getting it to market. This is exactly why they *do* like the exotic viognier, a wine that demands to be bottled fast and drunk the same year – the perfect cash-flow wine, a wine for the accountants.)

At Calera "yield" has another set of referents altogether. The yields have been absurdly low by the already low standards of Burgundy and other high-end producers. That these low yields produced superlative wines is a cause-effect calculation that has yet to be finally revolved.

Calera's low yields were caused by drought, lack of natural water, bureaucratic harassment, lack of nutrients in that limestone soil, pests, stress and inadvertence. And probably by bad (or good, depending on your perspective) karma too.

In Burgundy, the "magic number" for a yield is 45 hectolitres per hectare, above which most *premiers crus* require declassification. However, yields can vary for "good" wines (as opposed to "great" wines) anywhere from 50 to 100 hectolitres per hectare without greatly affecting quality. In the more fertile fields of California, and under the Western sun, it's quite common for table grape growers to reach seven or eight tons of grapes per acre. With healthy vines, four tons per acre can yield first-class wines, though some producers say anything over three won't do.

At Calera, three tons would be a miracle.

In the second year of the drought, the second year of producing single-vineyard pinot noirs, the yield was a pitiful half-ton per acre. Since then, Calera has struggled to reach two tons per acre. Which is why the '92 vintage, achieved with "average" rainfall rather than the meagre water of previous years, was so extravagant by Calera standards.

"Mind you, we also gave our vines lots of fertilizer that year, and that significantly improved our yields. It proved our land needed nutrients, not just water. The 1992 rainfall was just average, and we got terrific yields, a record in five of our six vineyards – 2 tons per acre on the Jensen, Selleck and Reed, 2 1/4 on the Mills, 3 1/2 in the chardonnay, and 4 in the viognier. Only the Jensen has had a better year, and that was in 1987, when we got 2,178 cases from it; this year (1992) we'll get 1900." The 1990 Jensen was from a typical Calera yield: 975 cases of wine were made from the 14 acres, a driving-bankers-to-distraction yield of about one ton an acre.

The crop averages for the named pinot noir vineyards are 1.53 tons (23 hectolitres per hectare) for the Reed, 1.42 tons for the Selleck, 1.54 tons for the Jensen, 1.33 tons for the Mills, and (a two-year average only) a piffling 0.58 tons for the brand-new Ryan.

For the first six years, the single-vineyard pinot noirs carried another line on their bottle labels: Young Vines. The Mills, chardonnay and viognier vineyards, which were planted in 1984, only dropped the designation in 1990.

Grape growers date vines by "leaf," not in years. That is, they count each growing season. Vines planted in July are one leaf vines in December and two leaf vines the following December (not one and a half years). First leaf just means they've gone through one growing season. Third leaf – that is, the end of the third growing season – is the earliest a vine will yield a decent crop. Wines from young vines usually have less concentration, less stuffing and less body.

The converse is also true – the older they get, the more concentrated the finished wine. On the other hand, yields drop. You get fewer and fewer grapes and the wine becomes greater and greater. Jensen gets positively dreamy contemplating venerable vines. "The very oldest vines, vines 120 years old, would make sublime wine, but you'd only get a few bottles per row. So in order to make a business of it you have to replant portions periodically. The standard commercial practice is to pull the vineyard out at age 40. I'm a contrarian, and I'd be inclined not to do that, but I'll be pushing up daisies by the time that decision has to be made. It won't be up to me. I like old vines but my children or someone else might want to take them out."

CHAPTER EIGHT

In which drought takes its toll,
a vendetta is conducted against
our winemaker in the matter of
water and costs get out of hand

 t doesn't rain enough in California, even when there's no drought. And when it does rain, it rains at the wrong times, in winter. So grape growers must perforce irrigate.

This drives the French to distraction. They're convinced that irrigation spoils the grapes – that it cannot possibly have the same beneficial effects as natural rainfall. They've even made irrigating vineyards illegal. Of course, that's all very well for them to say – most years they get far more rain than they need, and drainage is more important than moisture retention in French soil. Which is why the Burgundy sites that produce the best wines are almost always on well-drained slopes. (On the other hand, the French will readily toss bags of sugar into their fermenting wines to counteract overacidity caused by meagre sunshine. This "chaptalization" is illegal in California. In truth, even the French think there's something faintly disreputable about it, and hardly discuss it in polite company. To each his own adulteration.)

Most new grape growers in California install drip irrigation systems, and this is a source of further contention. Obviously, vines must have water, since overstressed plants won't produce a decent crop, but the French view is that if you deny a vine easy access to water you'll force it to root deep – 30 feet or more – and it will pick up interesting and flavourful minerals along the way. Irrigation, especially the kind of precisely controlled system practised at Calera, causes the roots to bunch near the surface, in the moist cone caused by the drip. A vine dependent on this shallow water won't need to go deep, and, or so the French maintain, it will lose access to all those interesting minerals.

Josh Jensen hardly enters this debate – without irrigation, his vines would die. He must irrigate or perish.

He does this in a simple way. A subterranean hose system leads from the water source – more on this in a moment – to the head of each row, where it then enters a smaller rubber hose less than half an inch in diameter. This hose is tied to the same wire as the vine's cordon, the lowest of the three trellis wires. There's one emitter per vine, and the emissions are controlled by head valves, which deposit about a gallon an hour, exactly where the roots of the vine await. The system is very sparing of water.

Assuming there's enough reservoir water in the first place, drip irrigation has another advantage. Water stress, which is viticultural jargon for drought, can be precisely controlled, and a nervy grower can even attempt what the academics are calling "deficit water management" – that is, rationing water at critical moments. Water is most essential at two points in the growth cycle – when the berries set after flowering, and when they turn colour; vines *must* have water at those times. Most growers who irrigate cut back after the grapes colour. At this point grapes simply store excess water, diluting the skin-to-juice ratio so essential to great wine. On the other hand, if the weather is very hot, the grape's ripening system will shut down for self-preservation, and it must be watered to keep it cool. Deliberately rationing water before *véraison* (colouring) will therefore slow the grapes' growth, and rationing it afterwards may, if one is extremely careful, encourage ripening without increasing cluster weight. By bungling the rationing you could also, of course, simply kill the bunches. It's high-risk management.

For the Jensen vineyards, and for our bottle of wine, it's not so much a question of whether to irrigate, therefore, but whether there'll be enough water to do it properly. Water has always been the biggest problem Calera faces.

The merits of Josh Jensen's long fight with a multiplicity of enemies is not our concern, but it isn't surprising that for years he felt beleaguered, because those enemies ranged from the natural forces of a six-year drought to a politically correct concern for mystical Indian custom and ceremony. In this volatile mix could be found an elderly Judas (Jensen's phrase), the "eco-terrorist stormtroopers" of the California wildlife service, and a secretive mining company that Jensen believed was slowly buying up land around him, with the intention of turning his precious mountain of limestone into cement and miscellaneous rubble. There was even a Hong Kong gambling syndicate in there somewhere.

The enemies list had by 2006 been torn up. One had died, a few of the others had drifted away, and a truce of sorts was reached with his neighbour, who had been the catalyst for the whole thing. Nevertheless, water supply was and still is a source of intense anxiety for Calera.

Of course all farmers complain about the weather. I learned this when I was just a kid, and watched the worry about water consume my grandfather's life. He'd stand for weeks on the earthen levee of his only reservoir, watching the levels drop, until the mud on the dam floor cracked in the heat. Then his market garden crops died and his animals starved. Every few years or so, though, he'd watch as the rains came in torrents and the dam overflowed, and the mud walls were swept away in flash flooding, waves of muddy brown water washing away the dreams of another year.

In any case, even in more benign climes than southern Africa it's a rural cliché that the current year's weather is always the worst. In Calera's case, this cliché has come to have considerable validity. If you ask Jensen about water, his face will turn grim. He will also talk without interruption for an hour, never repeating himself.

"Generally, the story of our vineyards is one of not enough water. It's a real limiting thing for us. The only exceptions were a few years after I bought the second property, in 1982. By early 1992, it was becoming critical. We were in the fifth year of drought. There are two small creeks running through our property, but there wasn't surface water in them for all of those years.

"The source of our water in the first years were two shallow wells we dug with a bucket rig alongside one of our creeks, but there was never quite enough. We planted most of our vineyards in '75, and went immediately into the '76–'77 drought, the worst in California for years. So for the second and third years our vines were in the ground we had back-to-back droughts, and there was not enough water to take proper care of them.

"The first year, when we only had 500 vines, I watered them by hand. The following year we put in our drip system, the source for which was those two little shallow wells. Our water tanks were two backyard swimming pools, the above-ground kind, about 20 feet across. I think they held about 12,000 gallons each. In hindsight I realize it was a false economy, but we didn't have a lot of money then. That was a cheap way to get a tank.

"We placed one of the tanks down the canyon from the two wells, and used a gravity siphon to shift the water. From there, we used a 50-gallon-a-minute pump to move it into the second tank a couple of hundred feet up. That second one was higher than any of the vines, and we could use gravity to irrigate the whole vineyard.

"What we should've done was spend another $15,000 or $20,000 to put in some sizable storage tanks, 20,000 or 30,000 gallons, and store up more water each time, giving the vines all the water they wanted. The wells would have filled those tanks, at least that first year.

"A reservoir already existed on the property when I bought it, dating back to the thirties. In 1982 we built three more small ones.

"There was no shortage of water then. In '82 and '83 we were afraid the rain was going to wash the old reservoir out. In '84, '85 and '86 there was plenty of rain, and water flowed down Harlan Creek as late as July 1. When we do get good rains we get a double benefit – the wells improve too.

"In May and June we'd irrigate our vineyards. Those good years, we'd use less water. Jim would irrigate one night and take the dam down half a foot, the next morning it would be back up over the spillway. You didn't see much visible surface water, but there'd be springs replenishing it.

"In '87 there was virtually no rain. What we did get soaked in gently. At the end of the previous season we'd pulled the pond down to two-thirds or half full. Then, in the winter, it didn't rain at all. The '87 season was itself a dry year, and we said to ourselves, it's a good thing we've got the water. So we pumped it all on the vines, and we got the biggest crop we'd ever had, 4,300 cases.

"But that winter was worse. We had emptied the pond by September of '87, and nothing went into it in '88 – you could walk across the bottom in your best shoes, across all four of the reservoirs. We had a 75 per cent decline in our crop that year. We really got clobbered.

"On the advice of an old coot hereabouts, a man who had for years posed as our ally, and in fact had asked me once to name him as our agent for the State Water Board, we dug a little box spring lined with redwood planks in the creek bed, up higher than our reservoir, and we got what looked like a bonanza – 20 gallons a minute out of an eight-foot deep box. Still, by June and July of '88 our vines were looking like they were going to die. We had tiny amounts of water, and we had to husband it until the summer, and the two shallow wells were dry as a bone because the water table was down.

"By the end of the '88 year, we were down to five and then three gallons a minute. That kept 48 acres of vineyard alive. Three gallons a minute around the clock comes to a surprising amount of water, but it was still like going around with an eyedropper. We had only 1,300 cases of wine that year. Very intense, overconcentrated wine, tasted more like late harvest zinfandels than pinot noirs. It was pretty scary."

We were sitting in a restaurant in the little village of Tres Pinos, near the Cienaga Road, demolishing steak-and-salad and a bottle of Calera's Jensen '87 pinot noir. There was a noisy party of locals in the corner, but Jensen's anger easily carried to the tape recorder, balanced, ironically, against a water jar at the corner of the table. He thumped the table, making the cutlery dance, spilling a few drops of water. He didn't notice.

"You've got to understand," he said, leaning forward and waving his knife. "For the six years of the drought our ponds had been dry. But it wasn't just us. Remember, this drought affected not just the Gavilan Mountains. It was true of L.A., Idaho, Utah, most places in the Western U.S.

"Most of these places had the sense to admit there was nothing they could do about it – you can't just make it rain whenever you want. Our neighbours downstream are the only ones in all the West to know exactly what causes their water shortage – it's that SOB up on the hill, Josh Jensen.

"They didn't think their low water had anything to do with years and years of drought, oh no. They didn't accept that if a waterfall dried up it might have something to do with the fact that it hadn't rained for seven years. Oh no, no, no. They didn't understand that ground water, particularly, is like a bank account: you can't draw out more than there is. They blamed me, and they didn't want me to be able to store any water at all because of that. They filed protests. Our opposition was figure-headed by a Mrs. Ann-Marie Sayers, a half-Indian woman who said we had stolen the waterfall she wanted to use for Indian ritual purposes. She claimed she wanted to develop the site as a heritage area, and was going to build an earth lodge and a sweat lodge to accommodate these ceremonies. She hadn't noticed that her water had stopped because one of her horses had stepped on the pipe and crushed it . . ." Jensen rolls his eyes and grimaces.

"In November 1990 the State Water Board bureaucrats investigated. They found a couple of technicalities, but essentially said we were using water efficiently, and that the water we used wouldn't have gotten down the canyon anyway, it would have disappeared through evapotransporation.

"This didn't satisfy our neighbours. They kept at us, and in July 1991 there was a second report by one Katherine Mrowka, which was a real chamber of horrors. She simply accepted every argument they made, no matter how spurious, and rejected every argument we made. She rejected all our operating assumptions, and essentially said we didn't have the right to take or store water."

Nevertheless, water is subject to tripartite jurisdictions in California, and there were some sources the bureaucrats couldn't touch. The most secure source is ground water, because landowners have the absolute right to take that, so Jensen concluded that he'd have to drill several new deep wells. He did so in the spring and summer of 1992.

"We were real careful where to drill them, too. We were determined not to get caught in the regulatory snare, and to abide by whatever regulations they could dream up. For instance, the wells were at least 100 feet from the nearest creek bed, we surrounded them with a concrete hermetic seal, we did everything we could . . .

"Those wells went down 900 feet and 1000 feet, and cost $50,000 each.

"Then you add the pumps, wires and pipe for another $12,000 a pop, and we spent $124,000 on those two wells.

"They are rated at 15 gallons per minute, which doesn't sound like a lot but when you do that 24 hours a day for seven days for 12 months that's a million gallons, and that's a lot of water, particularly when you have, as we do, an efficient drip irrigation system. Eventually, we stored it in a large sealed steel tank, so we don't lose a drop.

"We have no electricity up there, so we must also have a generator. This costs maybe $23,000."

I started to add the numbers in my mind. The costs were incredible.

"Surely," I said, "if you told a grape farmer down in the valley that you have to use diesel fuel to pump water 1,000 feet and only get 15 gallons a minute, and this from wells that cost more than a hundred thousand, he'd have you committed?"

"Yeah, sure," he said. "But given the rarefied pricing of our wines and the high economic value of our pinot noir, it's acceptable for us. Just."

"Was that the end of it?"

"Not at all. We had to hire a geo-hydrological consultant to tell us where to drill the wells, and he cost $50,000."

"Seems a bit steep?"

"Yeah, well, what you gonna do? Our legal bills were $50,000 and running. We had to hire a water engineer. He cost $35,000. Eventually, to fight off the endless numbers of bureaucrats, and to get the endless numbers of permits we needed, we had to hire: our own biologist, to prove we didn't destroy habitats, our own archaeologist, to prove we weren't desecrating a sacred site, our own soils engineer to inspect the compacting of soil around the dams was adequate, and on and on . . . it was insane.

"Our total water bill *for 1992 alone* was over $300,000."

There were four small reservoirs near Calera's vineyards, and prior permits allowed Jensen to store 22.4 acre feet of water (an acre foot is about a third of a million gallons). These permits, too, were being attacked, and in an effort not to be stripped of those, he finally stopped representing himself and hired a top water lawyer. On May 27, 1992, they met, with witnesses, opponents and all, and got an agreement – sort of.

Calera agreed to abandon two of their four reservoirs, but received the right to rebuild the largest and construct another, smaller, reservoir between the Selleck and Reed vineyards. But both those reservoirs had to be constructed with a drainpipe, and Calera could only add water to them between October 31 and March 31, and then only if there was aboveground water in the creek all the way through Sayers' property.

By the end of 2005 their secure supply was one reservoir of ten acre feet but which was full only one year in three, one large 100,000-gallon storage tank, filled from the two deep wells, and two shallow wells that could only be used, according to the agreement, when the stream was flowing strongly.

By February 20, 2006, the main reservoir was less than a third full. It's a truism of the climate that 80 per cent of the annual rainfall happens in January and February, so if you got to the end of February without "proper" rain, you probably wouldn't get any. Certainly by the end of February he was start-ing to get anxious. "Napa and Sonoma are 300 per cent of normal this year because they had gigantic rainstorms over New Year, but we didn't get that. We did get some rain, but it all soaked in. The dam is dry and the creek isn't flowing. It is going to be a difficult year." Still, in mid-March the rains came. Not copious rains, but enough.

To build the second reservoir, he figures, would cost maybe $130,000 or $140,000. "Jim [Ryan] and Diana [Vita] and our water lawyer think we'd be better off drilling two new deep wells for the same money. I'm the only one who likes the reservoir." He sighed. "In any case, we need to pay off some bank loans first. By that time we will truly have pondered the decision, and hopefully will make the right one."

This story of acrimony and contention, this anxious wresting of water from parched ground and permissions from desiccated government procedures, is all part of the particular history of our bottle of Calera Jensen pinot noir. I drank a glass or two of the '92 the night he told me the story, but of course tasted none of the bitterness and anger of the fight to keep the vines alive, none of the worry. I suppose the same would have been true years before, when as a child I ate a bowl of my grandfather's strawberries, produced at such cost and such anguish and such stress, after a year of savage dust storms in the interior of Africa. Then, I tasted only the fruit, and the warmth of the sun. Now, I went back to my room in San Juan Bautista and ate a piece of dried beef with my Jensen pinot noir. It seemed to me the wine tasted faintly, faintly, of violets.

CHAPTER NINE

*In which the grapes that will
make our bottle of wine are
beginning to ripen, sweeten and
swell under the California sun*

 y March, the shoots that will eventually make the following year's wines start to swell – small round green buds like little lymph nodes, just below where the current year's leaves and flowers are sprouting. By summer, when the canopy is in full leaf, the small nodes are mostly hidden by the foliage. They remain there all season, not swelling any further, soaking up what sun the leaves allow. The crop in 1989 was small, pitifully small; the bunches of grapes were tight-set, the berries smaller than usual, widely spaced on the canes. The vines were suffering from severe water deprivation; it was the worst year of the drought, and Calera was not prepared – its creeks and reservoirs dry, it was subsisting on minuscule amounts of water from the small hole dug in the creek bed, no more than three gallons a minute

to water 48 acres of vineyards. There was a 75 per cent drop-off in the crop. The nodes that were to make our wine did nothing. They simply waited their turn, the following year.

The harvest in September was subdued. Jesus Zendejas hired fewer pickers than he normally would – there just weren't enough grapes to make a full crew worthwhile.

The nodes were left on the canes after the pickers went through.

Then, in the pruning, most of them got cut off. That was quite normal.

The harvest is the death and life of a cycle in the vineyard and in the winery. The grapes have gone to the crushers and the vines look forlorn, empty; they are still in leaf but the fruit has gone. If there's any downtime in the vineyards, it will be in November and December. When he was younger and not responsible for a crew, Ryan used to wish for a soaking wet November. "There'd be no reason to go to work, because you just couldn't get there." He laughs. Life is more complicated now. Those of his crew being paid by the hour hate rain; the enforced idleness means they don't get paid. By contrast, the vineyard manager hates rain because he's paying men to do nothing. Rain means chores don't get done. On the other hand . . . rain means the reservoirs begin to fill, perhaps even the creeks to run.

But the fall of 1989 was, once again, dry. So Ryan organized his crew for what he calls "slack time, but not downtime." His reduced crew had been working, literally, seven-day weeks for five or six weeks or more, and they needed to catch their breath. Some of them he let go fishing. "Take a couple of days in November as 'summer holidays.' Then they get Christmas and Easter vacations – that's also time to relax, take trips, because they don't get to take trips in summer."

It wasn't as if there was nothing to be done. In the second week of November there was an infestation of gophers, and Ryan assigned a man to set traps. Gophering is a full-time occupation on Mt. Harlan; the brazen pests never seem to have downtime themselves, and they're a menace to a well-run vine-yard. His crewman would stay up in the vineyards for a week, setting and emptying the traps, patrolling the perimeter with his shotgun. And while he was there, he dealt with other rodents, with rabbits, ground squirrels, rats . . . all the many creatures that would feast on young vine shoots in the spring.

There were also a few holes in the fences. Deer, constantly pushing, had broken through in spots. They're a problem in the spring, when they damage the fresh foliage, and they have to be kept out. Some of Calera's fences are in the bush where they are hard to find and hard to maintain, and constant patrols are necessary.

There's machinery to be serviced in preparation for the next year. There are tractors, sprayers, dusters, disks, harrows, pumps – dozens of pumps of varying capacity to be checked and stored. There's never quite enough machinery. Farm managers regard agricultural implement showrooms the way a computer hacker does a new products expo; there's always some marvellous new and very expensive toy that, if only we had it, would make our lives that much easier and us more productive. (The seductive part of all this is that it's true, if hardly cost-effective.) Well, so there's maybe not enough machinery, but there's plenty enough to need maintenance. The equipment has to be put away for the winter, greased and stored. Pumps have to be winterized. There are always construction projects on a farm. Maybe build a new tool shed, another barn, a pump house . . .

That year, Ryan's crew took down the pumps and irrigation system early. There was no water, in any case, and they might as well do the maintenance while they had time. They tore down all the main junctions and connectors, dismantled all the pumps, checked the main irrigation lines, and checked the 45 miles of hose with their 40,000 drip-emitters to see that they were performing adequately.

In 1998 Calera stopped using artificial fertilizers and non-organic pesticides and herbicides. The following year they had to relent a little after an infestation of nematodes, but that was the last time. After that they tried feeding a compost tea through the drip system, but it plugged the emitters. They still deliver some gypsum through the drip system, which helps open up the soil and make it more porous to water, besides bringing the pH down and adding calcium to the soil.

Ryan likes to let the vines go for at least a month before starting the pruning. Pruning seldom starts before early January. It must be completed before the first buds swell, which will be sometime in March, and generally the crews aim to finish by the end of February, or mid-March at the latest. Four to six men move into the vineyards with their clippers. Each man prunes a couple of rows a day, and by the time it is done each has pruned well over 7,000 vines, squeezing his clippers maybe 70,000, 80,000 times, possibly more. The cut ends are dropped between rows, to be picked up later, mulched or burned.

Until recently, Calera vines were trained to a three-wire trellis. In the winter each was cut back severely, leaving just the trunk and the two "cordons" spreading three feet on each side (almost touching the next vine, some six feet away). These bilateral cordons were attached to the bottom wire. On each cordon the pruners left six spurs, growth from the previous season. Six spurs on each side, each spur cut back to 2 buds, 24 buds per vine. The shoots from those buds will grow up towards the sun; they'll either catch the wire above, or the crew will tie them up later. The pruners now select the most vigorous shoots on the trunk itself, fan them onto the trellis wires, and tie them down. They'd still aim to leave somewhere between 24 and 30 buds, depending on the vine.

Pruners have some discretion here. If the wood from the previous year looks particularly healthy, the pruner may leave an extra 10 or 12 buds on extra spurs. This will add considerably to the eventual crop. A spur the size of an ordinary pencil is the smallest that will carry 2 buds. Anything smaller is generally cut to 1. Anything larger . . . as long as the spur looks healthy, if it's round, with clean, long buds, and a little thicker, the pruner will leave a few extra buds. It takes experience and a good eye.

In the early weeks of 1990, the buds looked healthy, normal. The stress on the vines hadn't made for weedy spurs. But there were no extras either – 1990 would not be a massive crop.

By March 13, the pruning was done.

One of the men was sent through the vineyards with a mower, to chop the prunings and the brush so the disks and the harrows and the hoes could get through.

Between the rows, cover crops, usually peas or other legumes, are planted, and disked into the soil when they are mature as soil builders and to add nitrogen. Disking will be done four or five times in a season. To control weeds under and between the vines Ryan uses a spray of vinegar or a mild soap, and hoes by hand.

Once a year he dusts with sulphur, another natural product, to control mildew. "That's the only thing I treat for right now. Some years you get one problem, another year another problem. Our main problem is mildew. In the valley, in Salinas say, they've got mildew, fungus, bugs, everything. Of course, they spray-irrigate, which leaves water on the vines and the clusters, a perfect environment for bacteria and viruses that grow on vines. So every time they water they have to go back and spray. Drip irrigation just doesn't cause as many problems. And down in the valley, and near Monterey, if one farmer gets a pest, the whole damn place will get it soon enough, they're that close together. That's one of the good things about our vineyards, their isolation."

The few weeks between the swelling of the buds, in March and April, and the close of the "rainy season" (if there is one that year), about mid-May, is the time in the cycle when the crop is most vulnerable to frost. This is perhaps the single most anxious period in a grape grower's calendar. The only moment in the winery that could compare with the fear of frost is the fear of a stuck fermentation – that moment when the fermentation, for no apparent reason, simply stops, leaving the winemaker with a large tank full of sugary, half-fermented muck.

The sweet green growth of April is particularly vulnerable to frost; it hasn't had time to grow itself a protective sheathing, and it's still reaching eagerly for the sun. I've heard hard-bitten vineyard men, many of them as "ornery" as Josh Jensen's vineyard workers, wax lyrical about these tender green shoots; they became as worried as the father of a young girl on her first date, and if the date goes wrong, if the abusive hand of Biker Frost damages the young thing, they react with the same pathetic mixture of useless anger and violently protective concern. The worst time of all is when the vine is just about ready to set fruit – the cold will hit the young clusters hard.

In all their 30 years, the Calera vineyards have not – yet – had a killer frost, and although the elevation protects him to some degree, Jensen is realist enough to know he's going to get one in time. There have been serious frosts in parts of California as late as June 1. If Calera does get hit, Jensen has no defence.

"Our specific site up there doesn't have much frost, knock on wood. When I put in those first 500 vines, that was one of the things I wanted to know. I needed to know if they were going to be destroyed by rogue frosts. Well, nothing happened.

"If it had, I couldn't have done anything about it. I still can't. We don't have frost-protection technology. We'd be dead ducks."

There are two main ways of defending vineyards against frost. Smudge pots – smoky fires that warm the air a degree or two – are used mostly in Europe. The main technology in California is, somewhat surprisingly, to spray water on the vines. It's the same treatment Florida citrus growers use.

The physical principle is simple enough – ice won't drop below 32 degrees F, zero C, if there's unfrozen water on the surface. So those growers with spray irrigation systems (and lots of water) turn on their sprinklers when the frost alarms go off, usually at about 4 a.m., and the sprinklers go on spraying water until the danger is over. The grower ends up with icicles, but so long as the pump doesn't give out or the water doesn't run out, the tender green shoots won't be damaged.

The protective window is very small – the shoots are safe to 29 degrees F, and the ice won't drop below 32 – but it's enough, all the vines need.

However, Calera has neither sprayers, nor the right pumps, nor anywhere near the amount of water needed. "Fortunately, we've never been really hurt by frost. There's always one part of the vineyard that gets a little bit burned, but it seems to be a different part each year, and the section that got hit last year will be all right this year. The crop may be reduced somewhat in those sections that are burned, but not seriously. Of course one of these years we'll have a great big one, that's inevitable. I always figured that once we got into it we'd have one in ten killer frosts, one year in ten would be a wipeout or big-time loss, but we're in better shape than that."

Vinifera vines are not vulnerable to dormant-season frosts, or at least the kind that California produces. The only potential problem would be with the freezing of water lines, but by the end of December all the irrigation lines have been drained, and the mains and main branches are all buried.

In the drought years, Ryan's crew had to contemplate cranking up the irrigation system even before the frost danger had completely receded. With adequate rainfall, as there had been in the early '80s, the creeks would be flowing and the ponds full, and irrigation wouldn't start until late May or early June. In the drought years, it would start in March or even in the winter.

In 1990, after the dreadful year of 1989, irrigation with what water there was began in late March.

Even when there is rain, they still irrigate. The basic rule of California precipitation is that it doesn't rain from May 1 to November 1. "When people who aren't used to California come here in the summer they'll say, boy, it looks so brown, you must be having a really rough summer. Well, there is never a summer when the hills aren't brown. In Burgundy, they get two inches of rain a month, winter or summer, and Mother Nature does the irrigation. We can't rely on that. We'd only get half a ton per acre without any irrigation whatever, with total dry farming, compared to the yields that are routinely gotten in Burgundy of three or four tons or more per acre. Even with our supplemental irrigation in the summertime we still get yields below that."

When Calera does irrigate, it irrigates very efficiently, and the actual amount of water delivered is small. From May to December they might deliver 50, 60, or 80 gallons per vine; the most they've ever done, even in the most desperate straits, is 100 gallons per vine per season.

Jensen's $300,000 investment in water gave him a secure supply – but then of course he went and nearly doubled the acreage planted, and was back to just enough water and far too much anxiety.

Through June and July, the crews train the vines, tying up the shoots to the second and third wires. They shoot rabbits, trap gophers and ground squirrels, hoe around the vines, and "sucker" the vines, removing the spontaneous growths coming up from ground level or below ground level. If these suckers were allowed to grow unchecked, the vine would be wasting much of its productive energy on growth that served no purpose. The pruners rub off suckers or sprouts on the trunk itself. Those from below ground are followed down to the underground wood system, where they're cut off flush with the trunk. Suckers start coming out again in June, when the vine is bursting with new life, and the crews go back and sucker again.

The intention is to make sure the vine concentrates on the right kind of foliage and on its fruit.

Once more in late June they go back to repair the deer fences.

Several times during the month they disk for weeds. After that, they go at it manually, with a hoe. There is usually a second crop of weeds in July.

In August, the red grapes "colour up." Most wineries take careful note of when this occurs; the process, called *véraison* by the French, is an important part of the season, and the French have developed rules of thumb for how many days it is from *véraison* to *vendange*, from colouring-up to picking. Calera takes notes too, but maybe not so carefully. Or in any case, their notes are not always followed very meticulously. At Mt. Harlan *véraison* needs to be tracked mostly because it's a sign that the percentage of sugar in the grapes is increasing, and when the sugar gets to be about 18 per cent soluble sugars, or what the winemakers call 18 degrees Brix, another of the Gavilan pests, the insatiable bird called the linnet, begins to take an interest.

For years, Ryan's crew would break out the shotguns again and go back into the field, trying to scare off the linnets and, where that failed, shooting them. This hardly ever worked, because the vineyards are so spread out and inaccessible. Still, they tried to scare them off before the start of the season, to get the population under control before they could do any real damage. Linnets are Robin-sized songbirds, and the summer cock can be a wonderful wild crimson, but they can eat truly stupendous amounts of fruit, up to half a ton an acre. When yields are four or five tons, this might be acceptable, but in Calera conditions of inadvertent stress management, half a ton can be half the crop and the difference between a profitable year and one the bankers will inherit.

When they converted to a more organic way of farming, the shotguns were left in their cabinets and bird feeders set out instead, filled with corn. Give the birds some choice, the theory went, and their damage to the vines would be smaller. It works, too.

From July to September, therefore, the Calera crews are fighting off (or feeding) pests and watching the grapes ripen.

The picking starts, usually, in September.

In 1987, for the bottle of wine that started all this, in the Jensen vineyard, picking started September 17, and lasted until just into October.

CHAPTER TEN

In which when to pick the grapes
is seen to be the most crucial,
and anxiety-inducing,
decision a winemaker must take

From the first of September Jensen and Ryan are in the vineyards every day, keeping a close watch on the grapes in all the parcels and sub-blocks, warily watching the weather and the toll the birds are taking.

When to pick is one of the critical decisions in the life of a wine, and Calera's vineyards, because of their different slopes and orientations, all mature at slightly different times. The vineyards face all four points of the compass; the western exposure is usually the first to ripen, and the north-facing hillsides the last. This makes harvest management easier – crews don't have to get all the acreage in at once. Another advantage: smaller, more flexible crews are needed. The number of pickers can vary from five to ten, depending on the timing and the size of the crop.

Picking can stretch over a full month, usually from September 15 to October 25, though it can vary on either side by several weeks. Calera usually picks later than even the coolest portions of Napa or Carneros.

The determining factor in the quality of the vintage is the grape's ripeness.

But when is the grape ripe? When the sugar levels happen to be high? Or is it more complicated than that?

Many winemakers believe that the timing must be very precise, and that particularly in warm climates the peak period for a crop may last only a few days. That happens only when the raw green tannins have matured and softened but before there's loss of acidity or the accretion of too much sugar.

There's also a debate between sugar-ripeness and "phenolic ripeness" – the notion that grapes can be sweet but not yet fully developed. This in turn is part of the current acrimonious debate about wine styles and alcohol levels. More of that in due course.

For millennia the traditional way to judge ripeness was to crush a grape in your hand; if the hand remained sticky afterwards, it was time to pick. There are still wineries in Burgundy and even in California who pick as much on flavour as sugar, on the taste of the grapes. Taste, however, is a treacherous measuring device, and takes great experience to bring off correctly. Grapes in perfect balance are difficult to judge – the acid will hide the sugar and the sugar will mask the acid, and it takes fine judgment to be able to gauge sugar content properly. Josh Jensen doesn't even try. He uses sugar as his main compass – but makes an analytic judgment, rather than an aesthetic one. "And then you have to weigh other factors as well. For instance, are the birds starting to get at the vines, is the fruit starting to break down? Pinot noir especially breaks down very quickly."

The pinot noir always ripens before the chardonnay, and the chardonnay before the viognier. Except in 1992, when there was such a heavy crop on the chardonnay that the viognier came in before it.

In early September, they take samplings from all the named vineyards and sub-blocks. The samples usually show low sugar, but indicate which vineyard is ripening first. In most years it's the Jensen, with its south-facing slope. In the 1992 harvest, the Reed vineyard, for some reason, ripened earliest. "It's usually the latest. I still don't know why this happened. I couldn't believe it. That's why we have only one picking of the Reed '92, not an early and late as we usually do. I kept saying, well, it can't be ripe. It's never been the first to ripen before, so I sort of held off the picking because I disbelieved the samplings from the vineyard. Many years, with the Jensen, we have four or five batch pickings, and with the Mills we have four or five too."

As the days go on, and the grapes reach 18 per cent or 20 per cent sugar, these samplings get more and more frequent. Josh and Corneliu take more and more frequent cluster samples. They work systematically, going through the vineyard diagonally, taking a representative sample – a big cluster from a vigorous vine, a small cluster from a non-vigorous vine, clusters from different parts of the shoots, from different places on the hillside, some from the top of the hill, some from the thicker soils at the bottom. They also know that afternoon readings are higher in sugar than morning readings, because during the day the vine is sweating water, whereas at night it soaks it from the ground. They are also careful to pick whole clusters rather than individual berries. Testing the juice of single berries is possible, but complicated. The berry's ripeness will depend partly on where it's located on the bunch: riper on the shoulder of the cluster, lower at the farthest end from the stem.

They drop the clusters into a five-gallon plastic bucket, load it into Jensen's van, and drive down to the winery lab. There they mash the grapes and taste the juice. It looks dreadful, like a purple soup, but it tastes sweet. Then Corneliu tests it for sugar content.

There are several sophisticated ways of doing this, and two very simple ones. Many winemakers use a refractometer, a device small enough to take into the vineyards. It needs experience to use one properly, because it measures only minute amounts of juice, and it's essential to make sure to measure a grape that really represents the acreage being tested. The refractometer is a metal tube rather like a small telescope, with a hinged window at one end. In the field, you squeeze the juice of a single grape onto this window, hold it up to the sun, and look into the eyepiece. Light refracts through the film of juice, the sugar content bending the rays, and casts a shadow across a simple-to-read scale.

Corneliu uses both the refractometer and the much simpler hydrometer. This is the most basic measuring instrument in chemistry. You simply pour the grape juice sample into a little jar and float the hydrometer in it – the higher it floats, the more sugar there is. The scale marked on its side will tell you how much.

Often, the first samples will show readings of about 20.4,

meaning 20.4 degrees Brix, or 20.4 per cent soluble sugar – not yet ripe enough, although the grapes taste sweet and show good colour.

They continue taking random samples for several more days.

In 1992, on September 17, the Jensen Block A tested at 22.5 Brix.

Jensen radioed up to the vineyard: Okay, let's start picking.

The sampling continued, and tests were made on all the vineyards. After two days, when they had picked eight bins of Jensen Block A, the winemakers radioed up to stop picking. "We want to wait a few more days for the middle picking," he told Ryan. "Let's start on the Mills tomorrow."

At Brix 24, picking on the Jensen resumed. Then it stopped again.

At 26, Jesus's crew picked the last batch. It was October 5.

The finished Jensen picking was in four blocks and three pickings. Blocks A and B were combined, Blocks C and D, and Early, Middle and Late pickings of A and B.

This is the way the data were later recorded on Vita's computer:

A&B Early 420 gallons 13.1 alc 3.66 pH
A&B Mid 720 gallons 13.4 alc 3.71 pH
A&B Late 240 gallons 13.6 alc
C 900 gallons 11.8 alc 3.60 pH
D 240 gallons 12.8 alc

The 14-acre vineyard yielded 15.63 tons of grapes. Yield per ton varied from 165 to 175 gallons.

Batch picking was an accidental discovery. "We got into multiple picking sort of organically. We evolved into it.

Sometimes we'd get sample readings from a particular block that seemed to indicate the grapes were ripe, that they were at 24 Brix, so we'd pick a morning or a full day, and find out later it was only 22. So we stopped picking. That would become our early batch. We'd counteract that with higher-ripeness grapes, at maybe 25 or 26, and we found that the sum, the combined wine, was in the end greater than its parts. There was vigorous green character from the early picking in the finished bottling, and some decadent, rich, almost overdone flavours from the late picking. Put all that together, and we found it added diversity and complexity to the wine."

In later years, after Sara Steiner left, Calera got away from this notion of early, middle and late pickings, but in 2005 they resumed. Jensen acknowledges that during the single-picking years Calera made some of its best wines. It is a debate that continues.

The picking is done by Mexican transient labour, as it is everywhere else in California. Jesus Zendejas is the foreman. "I've been through all kinds of different ways of hiring pickers," Jim Ryan says. "This is the best. Jesus is the foreman of all the labourers, the pruning crew, the other crews. He's full-time, works all year, and he brings in all the workers. I tell him I want five guys, he brings me five. I handle the paperwork, but he takes care of the labour."

Jensen says Jesus "has guys knocking on his door at his house all summer long, reminding him not to forget them when he's putting his picking crew together. People like working for Jesus. He's fair. He expects them to work. If they don't show up one day he doesn't hire them the next, and they don't work for him for very long." Some years the pickers are given daily employment for a month, but this is unusual. In 1990 they more typically picked for three days and then stopped for three.

The Mexicans pick by hand. The preferred tool is a curved knife, a specialized implement rather like a serrated carpet knife. They're razor sharp. The workers are always sharpening them on their stones.

They work fast, almost at a run. And quietly, except for the occasional shout, curse or laughter. Five-gallon plastic buckets in hand, they tear into the vines, and the grapes mound up with amazing speed. The full buckets are dumped into bins carried along on a low flatbed trailer dragged through the vineyards by a tractor. There are two half-ton bins on the trailer; when they're full, they're lifted with a forklift onto the truck that will take them down to the winery. The winemakers will keep the whites, the chardonnay and viognier, until the end of the day, and then press a whole load. The single-vineyard pinot noirs are dumped from the trucks straight into the fermentation tanks, each batch kept separate from the others.

Down in the Salinas Valley and near Monterey, grapes are now often mechanically harvested. Many wineries rely on machines to get the crop in quickly, particularly in flat, heavily cropped vineyards of extensive acreage. These machines operate by slapping or shaking the grapes off the vine with plastic beaters. They knock the grapes off the shoots, doing a good deal of damage to the vines in the process. The grapes drop down into conveyor trays and thence to a truck in the next row.

Jensen will have none of this. There are no mechanical pickers in Burgundy although, alas, "progressive" growers are now buying them in some of the lesser appellations of France.

Kermit Lynch, who of all the wine writers is most resolutely against new-fangled methods (he once said of himself that he sometimes felt more like a preservation society than a person in the wine business), wrote in *Adventures on the Wine Route* how disappointed he had been one year with the product of one of his once-consistent suppliers. Then he discovered why: the fellow had bought himself a mechanical harvester! "He was tired of dealing with pickers. You must feed them lunch every day, and then there's all the paperwork, because you must treat each harvester as an honest-to-god employee, paying social security to the government, taking out insurance on every one though they only work for a week. And, he believed, no one could tell the difference in the wine. But the wines were thin, without colour or aroma."

When Jensen buys grapes for his workhorse wines, the Central Coast pinot noirs and chardonnays, he specifies to the growers that he'll not accept machine-picked grapes. "A couple of years ago we got a couple of trucks of machine-picked stuff. It was pretty disgusting-looking. We poured it into the tank and it looked like soup, like mush. It didn't smell right. I'm simply prejudiced against it. Of course, if you have a two- or three-hundred-acre vineyard, you can't pick by hand. So we pay a premium for our grapes." In addition, Calera's vinification method calls for fermenting bunches whole, an impossibility with machine-picked grapes. Also, because the grapes are so damaged, they have to be picked at night to avoid too-rapid oxidation and to avoid the necessity of oversulphuring to sterilize the juice.

The truck from the vineyard stops at the barn level, the highest level of the winery. There it's unloaded by a forklift, which dumps the grapes into hoppers, the fruit sliding down a chute into the tanks, a level below.

From this point, the job of the grower is done. Now it is up to the winemakers.

CHAPTER ELEVEN

*In which our winemaker reflects
on the risky business of making
fine wine and on how dollars can
be even more elusive than quality*

ne day in the middle of October, Jensen and I drove to the Iron Horse winery in Sonoma to take part in an unusual tasting organized by Riedel, the Viennese glassmakers.

The night before, we'd talked about the wine business and other matters. We started the evening at Toraya, a sushi place in San Francisco's Japantown. Jensen has catholic, if slightly conventional, tastes in sushi, favouring concoctions with nuts and avocado. We finished a bottle of his Mt. Harlan chardonnay, which he'd brought with him, and then we repaired for dessert to another restaurant nearby, Café Kati, where I remember a marvellous warm pear tart on puff pastry, and Jensen's extravagant raspberry crème brûlée. He drank two glasses of port while he talked. I finished with a glass of Bonny

Doon's gewürztraminer ice wine. We talked for a while about his view of San Francisco as a smug, small, provincial town. Then, before the tape was on, he talked about how he'd undertaken to get viognier rootstock imported from France, a process that took 15 years and rekindled his passionate dislike of bureaucrats of all kinds.

"When I first went to Romanée-Conti, they told me I should come back a week later when the harvest would begin, so I went down to Château Grillet, in the Rhône, to help pick there. I took my pay in wine, in three bottles of Château Grillet, which is really the best of the Condrieu viognier wines. I had gotten to know viognier quite well. The great restaurant La Pyramide, run by the legendary Fernand Point, was in Vienne, more or less across the river from Condrieu, and he served a good deal of Condrieu and Château Grillet, and I tasted it there. At that time there were fewer than 100 acres of viognier in the entire world.

"So in 1973, when I got back to California, I looked around to see if there was any viognier plant material. This was even before I owned any land. I paid $75 to Davis and their plant bureaucracy, the FPMS, the Foundation Plant Material Service, which is a joint venture between Davis and the U.S. Department of Agriculture, to start importing viognier. There apparently had been some viognier in California in the '30s, but Davis had said about viognier exactly what they'd said about chardonnay — not recommended for growing in California because its yields are too low. They were then pushing very high-yielding grapes, like Thompson Seedless, which yielded ten tons an acre, but were garbage grapes. My $75 started the bureaucrat-to-bureaucrat daisy chain. The California bureaucrats contacted the Washington

DC bureaucrats. Our bureaucrats there contacted the French bureaucrats in Paris. The French bureaucrats there contacted the bureaucrats on the Rhône Growers Council, asking them if they'd let this happen, would they let viognier go to America? So the legal official plants went from the Rhône valley to Paris, from Paris to Baltimore Maryland, where they were propagated in a USDA quarantine plot to make sure there was no horrible fungus or virus or bug. Maryland finally sent them to Davis, and they started growing viognier there. In the meantime, a couple of people had come and gone who were the heads of the FPMS, and they had no record that I was the guy who started this thing in the first place. Every January I'd call up and say, do you have any viognier budwood this spring? And they'd say yeah we do, who are you? And I'd say I'm Josh Jensen and I started all this, and they'd say, I'm sorry, there's no record of you . . . you're not on the list. I said, I started all this! I paid $75! No, sorry, you're not on our list. Finally they said okay, we'll let you have some then. Two weeks later they'd call up and say, we found a little bit of virus on one leaf so we destroyed it all. They burned it back to the ground and let it grow back up again. They did this year after year. So in '83, I heard there was a source in Geneva, New York, so I and La Jota and Ritchie Creek all got it from Geneva in New York. There was no trouble getting the stuff in from New York. It wasn't strictly kosher, I guess – there is a California quarantine. But the people at Geneva just UPSed the cuttings to a nursery in Bakersfield and the nursery told me later their workers called the vines 'voyager.'"

He started to laugh at the folly of it. The whole thing took 15 years! Bureaucrats!

Ironically, the viognier plantings were not, initially, a

success. The original set of grafts didn't take. "We had some vines that we'd graft and regraft and regraft and they'd grow for a while and die, or never take. We planted in '83, grafted in '84, regrafted in '85, '86 and '87. We thought we'd get a crop in '87, but we only got about 54 bottles, and in '88 a little over 100 bottles. In '89 we had 304 cases, which was two and a half tons per acres. Once we did start getting a crop it's been our Mr. Regular, our biggest yielder, two and a half tons in the first year, then two tons, then two and a half, and occasionally as high as four and even five tons.

"So, by a complete fluke, when we finally got it to market in '89, it was suddenly fashionable! We found ourselves on the cutting edge! But there was absolutely no forecasting involved, no market research; I just happened to like the variety, and the FPMS jacked me around for 12 years until it became fashionable."

Bureaucrats indeed. He pushed a little dam of syrup around on his plate for a while, and then offered up another example.

"You know that we now have the Mt. Harlan viticultural area designation?"

I said I'd noticed it on the label.

"Well, I got that. Actually, we're the only producer in Mt. Harlan right now. Know how long it took?"

I said I didn't. But I guessed a month or more.

"Ha! We submitted our application in February 1989. It took them a year to get around just to reading our application and then almost another year for reviews and hearings, with final approval being granted December 17, 1990. We've been told we were lucky that the government moved so fast on our application. Seriously!"

"How do these VAs work?" I asked. "I can see why you want a specific designation. Any Burgundian who believes in soil and the primacy of *terroir* would want it. I know it's the Bureau of Alcohol, Tobacco and Firearms that governs all this, but ..."

"Isn't America wonderful?"

"But, what do you have to demonstrate to them? I've seen BATF described elsewhere as 'omnipotent and sometimes capricious.' How does it work?"

"You must be able to demonstrate to them that the region you want is coherent, makes some distinct sense both topographically and from a winemaking point of view.

"There are other rules too. They have more rules than you can imagine. Wines labelled with a VA must have 85 per cent of their grapes grown in the delimited area. VAs can be as small as several hundred acres and as large as several million."

Calera is entitled to use three VA designators: Central Coast (an immense appellation south of San Francisco, including Alameda, Monterey, San Benito, San Luis Obispo, Santa Barbara, Santa Clara and Santa Cruz counties; it's mostly used to identify wine produced from two neighbouring counties); San Benito (which begins two miles south of Hollister and follows the San Benito river for several miles; only 1,700 acres of the total 45,000 are vineyards); and Mount Harlan (which is only 7,440 acres total; Calera is the only winery in the appellation).

Jensen reached across the table and pulled out one of his mailers, in which he'd quoted a press release from the California Visitors Review on the new designation. He started to read: "Mt. Harlan is a rugged, remote, high elevation area in San Benito County . . . Blah, blah, blah . . . Presently there are only 48 acres of vineyard within this large area . . . blah blah . . . and those vineyard acres are all owned by the small prestigious Calera Wine Company of Hollister."

"Ha!" he said, interjecting some of his own commentary at this point. "Prestigious! Tell that to the Water Board!" He propped the mailer against a vase and read on: "A little known mountain range, the Gavilans form the watershed, and the dividing line, between San Benito County to the east and Monterey County on the West. The new Mt. Harlan area is entirely in San Benito County. This is a high altitude, and very rugged area that is mainly used for cattle ranching and for hunting wild boar and deer. The lowest point in the Mt. Harlan AVA is 1,800 feet above sea level, and the highest, the summit of Mt. Harlan itself, is 3,275 feet. Calera's 48 acres of vineyards are planted around the 2,200 foot level."

He tucked the mailer away in a pocket. "The first of our wines carrying the Mt. Harlan designator was the '87 Selleck pinot noir. Since ours are the only vineyards in the VA, for the next six years or so at the very least, and perhaps forever, the words Mt. Harlan on a wine label are a guarantee of the very lowest vineyard yields and, hopefully, the highest quality."

I'd noticed that the labels didn't say "Estate Bottled," as some other producers did. Jensen looked disgusted. "We can't, because of a government regulation that the winery must be located within the VA where the grapes are grown, and ours isn't. It's just outside. But if there are wines around that are more estate bottled I'd like to hear of them."

He laughed. "People often ask us why we didn't build our winery close to the vineyards. I point out that there are no paved roads, telephones or electrical service anywhere in the Mt. Harlan area. So . . . no fax machines, microwave ovens or refrigerators. How could you possibly make wine without fax machines for communicating with your customers, microwaves to heat up your burritos, and refrigerators to keep the beer cold during those long hot summer days?"

"What about winemaking as a business?" I asked him. "I mean, premium winemaking, not mass market stuff. Can you make a living doing this?"

He thought for a while before answering. I turned the tape recorder on.

"There are so many wineries now not making any money! This is an extremely capital intensive business, and right now numerous wineries are falling into bankruptcy. Some of the trouble is caused by an overcrowded marketplace. They may be doing everything right, but just can't get shelf space for their products. They just can't get the restaurants to take in yet one more middle-range chardonnay.

"Some of the problems stem from errors.

"Often, people get into the wine business for the wrong reasons. People buying or starting a winery not because they're passionate about it but to have an elegant lifestyle. It sounds so gracious! They build a beautiful house, a luxurious house. They do beautiful landscaping. They hire a chef, rig out a hospitality suite, hire a PR agent. They build a showcase winery. And to do all this they borrow a lot of money from the bank (in the period when banks were looking to lend money – now it's the opposite). So they have high overheads, high costs and a high debt load and can't sell the wine. They then learn a sad truth: premium wineries are capital intensive businesses that pay back nothing in the short run and sometimes nothing forever.

"It works like this. A doctor, a surgeon from San Francisco, wants a place in the country, so he buys a few acres up in the hills in Sonoma. Of course, he meets his new neighbours and after a while they say, you should put in some vineyards, this is really good land for vineyards here. And so he does, he plants 40 acres of grapes. He sells them to say Robert Mondavi or the folks at Sonoma-Cutrer. But his neighbours aren't satisfied. They tell him, you're being ripped off by Mondavi (or Sonoma-Cutrer, or whatever), why, they're only paying you $15,000 a ton, that comes out to $3 a bottle and they're selling that wine for $18 a bottle and you should be getting that eighteen bucks a bottle, instead of the three, they're ripping you off, Joe. You should start a winery like the other people around here, and then you could be a winery owner and you could talk about your own wines.

"And so the poor doctor – or soon to be poor doctor – does that, and suddenly finds himself having to figure out all kinds of new things, all of them with large-dollar numbers attached. He has to find distributors. He's got to get himself a winemaker. His winemaker tells him he's got to buy 200 new barrels each year, at $660 a barrel, and that's $13,000. And suddenly he finds himself in a position where he's losing money every year, year in and year out, $100,000 in a good year, $200,000 in a bad year. And his problems are structural and unfixable. It's a crowded marketplace and Joe can't just raise his prices. He's got boxes stacking up in the goddam warehouse, so he's got to cut and discount and deal. Soon he tries to sell the winery, but who wants a losing winery making mediocre chardonnay? So his Arcadian dream has led to bankruptcy. And the Gallos get the winery. They only want it for its vineyards, and they get it practically for nothing.

"There's so much discounting going on right now! We recently turned down a 200-case order from a big-shot retailer in Sacramento. We got a phone call from our California distributor, and she said this retailer wanted to feature our wines through the Christmas season. Now, for a 200-case piece of business you could take a little something off, but he started trying to nickel and dime us down. It's the nature of today's marketplace. Joe and wineries like his have no choice but to go along, because they have bank payments, property taxes, they must fulfil their payroll, and they just don't have enough sales revenue coming in.

"We were able to say, okay, that's it, sorry, we thought you wanted the wine, but . . . we rejected the order."

How did Jensen avoid all those traps? His mournful face dissolved into a grin. He demolished a scaffolding of spun sugar surrounding his crème brûlée before he replied.

"How did we avoid all that?

"First of all, I managed to keep control of the winery. That's one of the many hazards in a precarious business, that you need money so badly that someone else ends up with control of your operation. Well, I've got news for you, this wasn't a hazard for us. Because no one wanted any part of Calera. It was considered a mongrel operation in a no-name county, and no one would invest in it. Even in the Bay Area people didn't know anything about this place. Mention San Benito in San Francisco and they'll barely know where it is. Mention Hollister, and they'll say oh yeah, Hollister, that's in earthquake country, isn't it? Or they'll say Hollister, isn't that by Eureka? They've heard of it but don't really know where it is. What we had were vineyards producing uneconomically low yields, we were making a variety that was considered to be impossible to do well in California then, we had people, even family and friends, saying I'd lose my shirt and make a fool of myself over this.

"The standard rule of thumb in the California winemaking business is that you lose money for ten years. And that after huge capital expenditures – vineyards, tanks, barrels, bottles, everything you need. The accountants will put those in the capital column and you can get depreciation from them, but the rule is that you lose money for ten years. I was getting money from anywhere I could beg, borrow or steal it. For ten years a little loan here, a little loan there, pledging whatever I could in collateral.

"That conventional 10 years was about 12 for us – we bettered it, if that's the appropriate term, by about two years.

"There were many, many, many times when it was just so discouraging. It would have been easy just to toss in the towel. But, during those dark and discouraging years, through the middle '80s, the assets in a fire sale wouldn't have begun to cover our debt. I'd have ended up wiped out, unemployed, discredited and branded a failure. So I never did come really close to throwing it in.

"The worst times were at tax time. Now, I never really pay much attention to profitability – I'm not a businessman, an MBA business hotshot type. I operate my business on the basis of personal relationships and a lot of intuition. And so what I've always looked at is our cash flow. In other words, do we have any money in the bank? Can we pay those guys this week or do we have to wait until next? There've been long periods in our history when we were just not at all prompt at paying our bills. We'd borrow from Peter to pay Paul. We were really struggling. Every April the accountant would mail me the tax returns, and I'd ask him, did we make money last year? And he'd say, no, no, we lost $80,000, $100,000, $60,000. We got into '84, '85 and '86 and I'd say, god, when is it ever going to happen? And he'd say, well, just keep going, you'll get there in the end. But it was in that tone of voice, you know, it sounded like he didn't really believe it.

"I remember at one point going over the numbers with my mother, who was then one of my partners, and her accountant, an absolute numbers guy, the kind of guy who didn't very often venture outside his office building in Oakland.

"He mumbled and aahed, and he said, well, let me see if I've got this right, your sales are so and so, and your interest payments are so and so and your net loss for the year was so and so, $60,000?

"I said yes, that sounds right.

"And he said well, pardon me if this sounds blunt, but this doesn't look like a very good business to me.

"And I said well, you've said it in a nutshell.

"And he said, so why are you doing this? Why don't you just sell it?

"And I said well, um, I've just gotta do it, and it's gonna get there at some point."

I was reminded of something George Bain, the late Canadian political commentator and wine writer, had once said: "Running a boutique winery is like joining some religious order fanatically attached to the idea that expiation is achieved only through unremitting toil."

"Yeah," Jensen said, "I can't say it wasn't discouraging, too. I mean, it would be discouraging even if you were among the mega-rich. You still don't want to lose $100,000 year in and year out. It just feels bad. When you're broke, and you're still borrowing some more and going around and eating crow.

"I guess that's the compulsion that entrepreneurs feel. It can unhinge a person. I've seen it in some people I know.

Personal friends as well as some of my distributors. They get to where they get delusional, separated from reality, and persistence becomes obsession.

"In my case, I just gambled. Pinot noir was immensely unfashionable when I started. Everyone was saying, not only was California pinot noir terrible but it always would be terrible. That was the perceived wisdom. So of course when I planted in that first go-round I planted all pinot noir. The gamble was this: I was tasting some pretty good chardonnays at the time, but no pinot noirs that were even interesting, so a successful pinot noir would be great news. So I put all my chips on pinot noir. I was young enough that I didn't realize I couldn't do it, so I just did it. I just went ahead. I was too dumb to realize I couldn't.

"Now of course they want to know how I knew that pinot noir was going to become fashionable in the '90s, and of course I didn't.

"At some point, though, you must return to reality. If the business really isn't going to make any money, persistence is just delusion. Every year we'd lose money: in '84, $80,000, in '85, $50,000, in '86, $40,000. The losses were getting smaller, the trend was right, but still we'd find ourselves saying, well, we sold a lot more wine this year, why didn't we make money? Then, in '87, we made $125,000 profit. I didn't find this out until '88, and I was dumbfounded when the accountant told me. We've been strongly profitable every year since. And that's with the stupid lousy drought that took away half of the highest profit part of our business.

"Why? I think partly because we acquired and developed loyalty with our distributors and marketplace people, and had gotten to personally know and win the respect of and make friends with retailers and restaurateurs all over the country, and our wines got better known. And suddenly, lo and behold, pinot noir started to become at least slightly fashionable, and we had finally emerged in many people's opinion as the best, or among the best in the country, and those who didn't think that we were the best we'd at least be on their list of top five. So our pricing finally got to the $30 area, and our workhorse wines sold for around $14."

Not that all this didn't test his nerves. Pinot noir is a notoriously fickle grape, and it certainly teased Jensen. His first crop in 1978 was only 75 cases. The Jensen vineyard gave him 2,200 cases in 1987 from a crop of just over two tons an acre, and the following year he got just 400 cases – from a crop of less than half a ton per acre. How do you run a business with that kind of unpredictability?

"There are wineries, miracle workers, who can show a profit in their second year. They don't own vineyards. They buy batches of wine on the bulk market, they put them out under a *négociant* label or brand, and immediately have sales revenue coming in. And if they buy smart, have a good product, and get a good launching into the marketplace, they can actually show a profit in their second year. There are guys who bootstrapped operations like that on a hope and a prayer, who have done an enviable job. One brand that comes to mind is called Stratford which is up in the Napa valley.

"But they are very much at the mercy of vagaries of the market. If suddenly there's a shortage of chardonnay, and they're known for $5 chardonnay, and suddenly the cost of chardonnay on the bulk market doubles, they don't even have a business any more. It not just that sales are down, they don't have a business at all. Because they can't convert those five-dollars-a-bottle customers over to ten-dollars-a-bottle customers."

Of course, it can work the other way too. Calera struggled for many years, but by 1990 was strongly profitable. Then came the harvest of 1992 – an extraordinarily large harvest for Calera. To put it into perspective, in 1990 Calera produced 3,000 cases of single-vineyard wines. In 1992, it was 7,000. The harvest was so good that for weeks Jensen just wouldn't believe the numbers coming in from the vineyard. They just seemed too high. As a consequence, the harvest brought in somewhere around $800,000 or $900,000 in incremental revenue, and that on a base of just $2 million. The incremental costs were additional labour to pick and then ferment the wine, extra barrels to keep it in, and packaging (around $15 a base for bottles, corks, capsules, labels, palettes, tissue paper for wrapping). But extra costs only accounted for about $100,000. The rest dropped straight through to the bottom line.

Of course, this whole discussion took place in the early 1990s. In the ten years following that the whole world of high-end wine changed, dramatically, twice – once for the better and once to near doom.

At first, the world of wine became red hot. In Napa and Sonoma and Russian River and Carneros and even down through to Santa Barbara, new wineries sprang up, and old wineries changed hands for astronomical sums. In the Old World, prices of the great Burgundy *domaines* went through the roof; Spain remade itself, Italy's Barolos reached prices beyond all but the rich. In the New World . . . South Africa threw off its bureaucratic noose and the legacy of apartheid-era boycotts to begin making wines to rival those of California; the

Aussies went on their great brand-making marketing binge, and in sleepy New Zealand winemakers could be found turning out sauvignon blancs and pinot noirs of quality. The Chileans and the Argentinians began to impose their presence on the marketplace too.

But it was a bubble. By the turn of the century there was already a worldwide glut of wine. On top of that, the Californians were faced with a stock-market collapse, the dot.com bust, the appalling aftershocks from September 11, and the collapse of the restaurant business. Wineries began to go bankrupt by the dozen; others brought in partners at ruinous rates; yet others sold to the Gallos at fire-sale prices and felt themselves lucky to get a penny on the dollar. The prices of Calera's high-end pinot noirs dropped from around $80 a bottle to the $50, $55 mark they were at in 2006, but overheads hardly dropped at all. The winery lost money for three years; all the staff took pay cuts and Jensen parked his Porsche, acquired in the boom years, in a garage, prudently out of sight and hopefully out of mind.

Those were fraught years. "Look," said Jensen, "it wasn't just here. The oversupply was worldwide. In France there was a huge lake of unsold wine, and other lakes in Italy and Australia and Chile. The California industry is healthy again" – here he tapped the wooden picnic table on Calera's terrace as he once again pondered the "life-saving" terrific year of 2005 – "but in California alone more than 100,000 acres of vines were pulled out, just in the last five years, and hardly any new vines planted. The French are much worse off. The super flagships are in good shape, but below those names, it's a bloodbath. The French often blame their lost sales on chauvinistic Americans, but that only explains 5 per cent of the drop. Their biggest problem, ironically, was health. A few years ago the French government lowered the acceptable blood-alcohol limits for drivers from 0.12 to 0.08, and at the same time cranked up the fines for drunk driving, and started confiscating driving licences and imposing jail terms. The results cut down on road deaths, but was catastrophic for the wine business. France makes the EU buy the surplus and distil it into alcohol, but it is a huge money loser. Also, both the French and the Californians are getting killed by the Australians. Their stuff is flooding in here at five dollars a bottle. I don't know how they can make wine that tastes so good and send it halfway around the world and still sell it at those prices. We can't do that.

"And in our market, sales dried up. When someone wakes up in the morning and sees his net worth has gone up by $20,000 overnight, he'll pay anything for a case of wine. But when his net worth has gone down by $20,000, $30,000, also overnight, suddenly he's looking for two bucks a bottle . . . And out of this comes Charles Shaw and his 'Two-Buck Chuck,' remnant wines he buys and bottles and sells for $1.99 in the discount marts . . ."

That, of course, was just after Calera had dipped into the banks for a two million dollar loan.

In the early years, Josh Jensen did all his own marketing. But when things improved, he hired a public relations agent, Ed Schwartz, to do his media and other contact work. PR went by the board in the Time of Troubles after 2001. "I guess we felt that was one big cheque we could do without writing, and we went naked for about three years. We were out of the news for a few years, and it may have been penny wise and pound foolish, but we just didn't have any money. Ed is back working for us now, and we negotiated an appallingly low fee, so low that he thinks he's working for free though for us it's still a lot of money. In any case, Ed is doing a good job getting journalists interested in Calera, and back in the news."

They didn't cut back everywhere. At the start of the bad years he hired a high-powered national sales manager, Marta Rich, an 18-year Robert Mondavi veteran, and it turned out to be money well spent. He has to expend more time than he'd like fighting off poachers for her services, but the 2005 sales figures are testimony enough that she's more than worth the price.

No doubt the hit movie, *Sideways*, helped too.

As we tooled across the Golden Gate Bridge on the way to the Iron Horse tasting, I asked Josh to tell me more about the early years of Calera, before his own vines were mature.

He'd finished planting his first three vineyards by the summer of 1975, but it would be a while before he could make wine from his own grapes. It wouldn't be until 1978 at the earliest, and then it would take another year or two before his first Young Vines wines could be released to the market. His own winery, the rock-crushing plant, wasn't ready until 1977.

Meanwhile, he wanted to meet other Californians who were producing pinot noir. He also wanted to find a way of making wine more quickly, and bring some cash into his business.

By an odd coincidence he found both fine pinot noir and space for rent just on the other side of the Gavilan range, where a winemaker named Dick Graff had set up his business and called it Chalone.

By another odd coincidence, Graff had spent some time

in Burgundy, and had met and been influenced by the great André Noblet.

Jensen sought him out. "Dick was one of the first people in the industry I met when I came back to California. He was then making *the* great California pinot noir, and when I tasted it, out of one of the barrels – and I mean, three or four barrels was what they were making – I said, well, so it *can* be done here. They were great wines, those late '60s, early '70s wines from Chalone. It was a small-scale operation, they were strapped for dough, living hand to mouth at that time, but they were doing it right. No redwood tanks for them. I learned a lot from Dick, who has, I think, also learned things from me because I had spent more time in Burgundy than he had been able to."

The Chalone vineyards were only a dozen miles away, if you were a crow, on the Pacific slopes of the Gavilan hills, and they were just as bleak, just as isolated, just as prone to wild temperature swings of 40 or 50 degrees from intense afternoon heat to chilly evenings, as Calera was to be. André Noblet's influence showed at Chalone too: the soil might be malnourished, rocky, poor – but it did contain limestone.

Like Calera, Graff had problems with water. Anywhere else Chalone's "vineyards" would have been classified as desert, and Graff resorted to drilling a well eight miles away on the valley floor near Soledad and running a pipeline up the mountainside. For the first few years Graff eked out a living in the hills, producing 500 cases of wine a year, without electricity, or even a phone line; when he needed to phone for supplies, he used the pay phone at nearby Pinnacles National Monument. In 1972 he found a partner, businessman Phil Woodward, and after a few years they had grown the business into Chalone

Inc., a publicly traded company that controlled, among other operations, Edna Valley, Carmenet and Acacia in California, and entered into a joint venture with Woodward Canyon in the Columbia River Valley in Washington. In 1989 Chalone struck a deal with the Bordeaux company Domaines Barons de Rothschild – managers of Château Lafite and owners of Château Duhart-Milon, La Cardonne, l'Evangile and Rieussec – which gave each company a 20 per cent stake in the other. The whole company was acquired in 2005 by the British-based Diageo, the world's largest drinks company.

By 1975, when Jensen needed them, Chalone had built a modern winery, but was only using a small part of it, so he rented space from Graff for his first two vintages. This was pure California; no French proprietor would dream of sharing space or equipment in the way California winemakers routinely did, and do. In California, winemakers shared everything from equipment to ideas with a candour that would have (and often did) amaze and appall French winemakers.

However, it wasn't pinot noir that Jensen made from his purchased grapes in this rented space.

"No," he said, making a face. "We bought zinfandel grapes. For our first three vintages, we made only zinfandel from grapes grown by others. So the first wine the Calera Wine Company made was zinfandel. I'd had this idea from the start – we'd make zinfandel to keep the cash flowing. It would be the winemaking equivalent of best-seller literature, and our pinot noirs would be the great books, to be supported by the best-sellers. We made zinfandel for 11 vintages, through 1985, before we discontinued it."

He was never tempted to plant zinfandel grapes on his own property. And the first year Calera made a profit, '87, was the last year he released any Calera zinfandel wines. The role that zinfandel had been supposed to play in the operation has since been taken by Central Coast pinot noir and Central Coast chardonnay, which Jensen calls his workhorses, his mainstay wines. "These are not inconsiderable wines – nor was our zinfandel – but our single-vineyard wines are a notch above that.

"In hindsight, the zinfandel experience was a big mistake, a strategic error. Hindsight shows zinfandel was starting an historic decline about then and the white wine boom was in its infancy. If we'd started out making chardonnay and pinot noir, we'd have had our first profit in '82 or '83 instead of '87. We could have ridden the escalator up to high prices, high margins, with much faster product turnover than we got with zinfandel. Zinfandel then as now had an upper limit, a ceiling, to its pricing. The top price for zinfandel is a mid-range price for chardonnay. And you have to hold zinfandel in the barrel longer than you have to hold pinot noir or chardonnay. Bad for cash flow."

In '75 he made a thousand cases of zinfandel at Chalone, and again in '76. By the '77 vintage, he'd bought his rock-crushing plant, and though it wasn't yet ready to make wine, he did make wine on his own property. "We made it up in a pole barn with open sides, which is now our tool shed and dry storage. We surrounded it with a barbed wire fence because it was open, and the bureaucrats required that a winery be lockable." He laughed. "Who was going to steal our stuff up there in the hills?" That summer they worked on the winery; engineers suggested he strengthen and buttress the original walls against earthquake damage. Then they added a fifth, and eventually a sixth, wall at the bottom, and enclosed those to be barrel cellars, a warehouse and a bottling room.

In 1978 he hired his first winemaker, Steve Doerner. Doerner had never made a bottle of wine before Josh found him, but that didn't matter. Josh wanted someone technical to help him while he went out to sell his zinfandel, and he wanted someone without any preconceived bias as to how wine should be made. Doerner had been a student at Davis, but he studied biochemistry, not enology. While they both searched for the simplest, most natural way of making wine, for the lowest possible tech, Doerner would do whatever chemical analyses were necessary to try to tip the balance to more hits than misses. (Doerner left Calera in 1992 for Oregon, where he was still making high-end pinot noirs in 2006 at Cristom estate.)

"That year, 1978, we made wine in our own winery, and the year following that I moved from the trailer over to my house. We were in business."

An hour or so later we turned into the driveway at the Iron Horse winery, located on 300 acres of rolling countryside in Sonoma's Green Valley. Iron Horse produces some pinot noir, but specializes in sparkling wines under its own label. The working buildings of the farm are small and functional, but the farmhouse is a gracious, rambling structure more than a hundred years old, surrounded by lovingly tended gardens. The tasting was held on a patio near the winery, a pleasant nook under an arbour overlooking the vineyards. The October sunshine was warm and golden. It seemed an idyllic spot, and an idyllic life. It was easy to see why urban refugees could be seduced into trying it.

Iron Horse was founded by Barry and Audrey Sterling. Barry was a San Francisco lawyer with a practice on both coasts and in Paris and a taste for the good life, almost as if he were the prototype for Josh Jensen's story of how to go broke making wine. Just as in the story, he fell in love with Sonoma's gentle hills and set about restoring a rundown property. However, he avoided the trap Josh had outlined, partly by making excellent wine. He also had the good sense to have a daughter, Joy, who became a winemaker of superior skill. She had the further sense to marry another winemaker of ability, Forrest Tancer, who also has his own winery, located on 450 acres in Alexander Valley. Iron Horse has recently gone into a joint venture with Laurent Perrier of France, and produces sparkling wines by the *méthode champenoise*, which sell at something of a premium price. (The *méthode* is *champenoise*, but the *technique* is pure America: the champagne bottles are given the careful and requisite 1/8th turn every few hours not by highly trained cellar workers but by a clanking machine capable of turning 400 bottles at a time. The bottling opera-tion, on the other hand, is curiously low-tech, and depends heavily on the ability of one of the workers to get his thumb over the bottle mouth with sufficient rapidity not to lose any wine as the crown cap is flipped off, the fermenting syrup inserted and the bottle corked.)

For this day Joy had brought together four premium producers of pinot noir, Acacia, Iron Horse, Calera and Saintsbury, at the suggestion of the Riedel glassware company representative, who had a point to make. The tasting was unusual in that we were not to compare wines, but the glasses they were poured into.

The glass, the Riedel person said in a little introductory lecture, is just another tool in the winemaker's armoury. He maintained that the "profile" of the glass, by which he meant its depth-to-circumference ratio, its capacity, and whether the wine pours from it in a wide arc or a narrow lip, all make a difference to the way the wine tastes. Different glasses will show, or mask, different characteristics of the wines, he said. Some glasses would bring out the acidity in the wine, some the fruit, depending on where in the palate the effect was felt and on the shape of the "pour." We were to drink the same wine from four different glasses, and make notations on a tasting sheet. Afterwards, we would see if he was right.

It's fair to say that his little lecture was received with a good deal of scepticism, though everyone was too polite to say so. They sipped diligently from the four glasses on the table – the Vinum Burgundy White (small and tulip-shaped, 12 3/8 oz.), the Sommelier's Montrachet (squatter, less tapered, 17 5/8 oz.), the Vinum Burgundy Red (more bulbous tulip, and bigger than the White, 24 3/4 oz.), and the Sommelier's Burgundy grand Cru (a 37 oz. behemoth that to my taste was clumsy and much too large, but which some of the others liked).

Everyone slurped and spat, pouring the surplus wine into the gravel under the bench. From time to time, they'd scribble on their sheets. Afterwards, we compared notes. My own tasting notes were far from precise, but to my surprise even I could tell that some wines did better in some glasses than in others. Most of the winemakers present were astonished, and while there was no real consensus, there was clear agreement that the Riedel man's notions had been generally right. What did it mean, though? That careful winemakers could move more product by stocking a wider variety of glasses in their tasting cellars? That yet another level of complexity should be added to the experience of consuming fine wines? Or was it just a curiosity, to be noted and forgotten?

Afterwards, we went to lunch at the main house, prepared by the winery's chef, and then set off for San Francisco and south, back to the Calera winery.

CHAPTER TWELVE

*In which the grapes come in
from the vineyard to start their
magical transformation into wine,
and in which techniques are described*

The grapes from the Jensen vineyard, Block A, went roaring past us down a stainless steel chute, and plunged into the open-topped fermentation tank, ten feet below. The Block B grapes would follow in a few days. I noticed a few leaves, though not many, and also that the berries were still on their stems.

A week or so earlier, at one of the California wine shows, I'd interrupted Jensen as an earnest young wine buyer was asking him about this business of stems. Did he de-stem at all? the young man wanted to know. If he didn't, were the stems woody-brown or green, and would that make a difference? Jensen was replying patiently, but I dragged him away, needing him for some other purpose. The young man glared at me.

Clearly, at least at that point, Calera didn't de-stem its grapes. There wasn't a de-stemmer anywhere in sight. I asked Josh what the orthodoxy on the matter was. The theory behind removing the stems was that they contributed too much astringency and bitterness to the finished wine if fermented with the grapes. He'd used a de-stemmer until 1984. After that, he just put whole bunches into the fermenter, not even crushing them, just punching them down a bit to break some of the skins. "I now think the de-stemmer bashes up the stems and extracts more astringents than if you leave the bunches alone," he said. In 2004, however, he relented and bought a small de-stemmer. Partly this was because of the high volume of purchased grapes for his Central Coast wines; but one of the new vineyard blocks made wines that were very tannic, and he wanted to experiment with de-stemming to see if that would make much difference.

Another bin went crashing past us into the fermenter. Eight feet or so tall, the tank was already about half full. He'd top it up a little more before moving on to another fermenter.

There's no consensus on this matter of stems. Dick Graff, when he was at Chalone, did as Jensen does, using whole clusters with the stems on. But Larry Brooks, the winemaker at Chalone's sister winery, Acacia, de-stemmed and crushed the bunches gently before fermentation starts, leaving about a quarter whole bunches. Tim Mondavi, at Robert Mondavi wineries, used to leave the stems on but has reverted to de-stemming; he believes the stems "give some spice to the wine, but dry them out too fast as they age." Kent Rasmussen, a young winemaker with his own eponymous winery, who makes some very fine pinot noirs, de-stems a little more than half the grapes.

"So it's not just Davis that says, take the stems off?" I asked.

He laughed. "No. Now, I don't . . ."

"I know," I said, "You don't want to be a Davis-basher, but . . . "

". . . want to be a Davis-basher at all. I'm not nearly as anti-Davis as I sound." This was probably true. When I talked to him in early 2006, he had actually been to the school, at their invitation, to deliver a lecture on his techniques.

We wandered down to his house, set on cascading levels down the steep hillside, and settled around a table on the lowest level, overlooking the rolling hills of the Gavilan range. I asked him to tell me what he really thought of the Davis school, and its theories of winemaking. Clearly, they'd done plenty of good for the industry, if only in the vineyards. Many of the techniques they had discovered, such as deep-ripping the land, and drip irrigation, were now routine practice in winemaking operations, including Calera. Their "foundation plant" sciences section, where they mutated, cloned and tested dozens of different grape varieties in small plots, had been derided by some winemakers as concentrating too much on yield and not enough on quality and flavour, but had nevertheless taught all winemakers much about plant biology and its pathologies – that California vineyards were as healthy as they were had much to do with Davis, the contentious recurrence of phylloxera notwithstanding.

The main quarrel with the school, as far as I could see, was the suspicion that since it was funded largely by massive Central Coast bulk wineries, the school's basic assumptions favoured high yield and consistency of flavour over character, nuance or "ageability." The emphasis was on mass production, on what the French call *vin technologique*. Everything had to be air-tight, squeaky clean. Kermit Lynch once wrote scornfully of some hapless winery that "the Invasion of the Enologists is [the horror film] now playing at their local cinema ..."

Josh Jensen agrees with this, though he gives it all a more charitable spin. "When Prohibition ended, most of the American industry had been locked up and shut down for 20 years, and to a certain extent they'd forgotten how to make wine. So the University of California at Davis was instrumental in fighting hard, and encouraging the industry to make sound safe wines and not vinegar through the meticulous application of the scientific method – primary chemistry, tightly controlled fermentation, meticulous sanitation and heavy filtration. They were adamant in taking very conservative, cautious approaches. In the large scale this was a good thing, because there were a lot of unsound, unhealthy wines. To their credit, the result was a preponderance of sound wines, cheap, homogeneous jug wines, but still sound.

"On the other hand . . . it was an interventionist form of winemaking, consistent with a basic belief that technology can solve all problems, and you just can't make great wine that way. Why? Because it pays no attention to the characteristics of the grape, or the soil, or to excellence or to the very idea of extraordinary quality." High-technology winemaking is salvage winemaking – it's for saving wine that has gone wrong, or was never very much right in the first place.

"So," I asked, "they believed if they understood enough of the wine's chemistry, that if they got just the right clone, the right fermentation temperatures, the right yeast strain, the right stainless steel tank and the right oak barrel, they could produce great wines?"

"Well, the school's mandate was not great wine. Their graduates, some of whom did want great wines, believed more in microorganisms than in character. So they never made great wines. They made some interesting wines, but not wines of the very first rank.

"Most of them, in fact, were wines that lacked colour, lacked complexity, and lacked character – safe and boring. This conservative approach will do this with whatever grape you're using, but especially with pinot noir."

It was left to the next generation of winemakers, such as Josh Jensen, to reject this notion of wine as some kind of malleable Pygmalion to be made over by white-coated Henry Higginses, and to rediscover the surprises and pleasures of minimalism, formerly known as nature. And minimalism – when to leave well enough alone – is an acquired skill. Anyone can make pretty good wine; to learn the patience of great wine takes a lifetime.

We wandered back up to the winery; another truckload of grapes was coming in from the vineyards, and Jensen wanted to be there. "Here's what I really think about winemaking," he said, ticking off the points on his fingers. "The grape essentially knows what to do. The job at the farm level is to get the grape to the perfect state, and capture it at that moment. And then the winemaker's job is to stand in the background, get out of the way, and let it get into the bottle as purely, as naturally, as possible, with as little done to it as possible. When in doubt, don't do it. Too much California wine is made from a standard recipe. It's why they had so much trouble with the pinot noir grape before. You can't treat the pinot noir that way."

I thought this doctrine of rigorous non-interventionism somewhat disingenuous, and said so. He looked sheepish.

"Well," he said, "there are times when you have to intervene. If someone gets a headache you have to give him aspirin. The point is, when in doubt, do as the Burgundians do, that's your starting point. And they do as little as possible."

We went back up to the fermentation tanks, and peered in. The tank was three-quarters full of grapes, most of them still whole, but a small percentage broken open. It smelled, of course, nothing like wine, but of crushed fruit and bruised wood.

"Okay," I said, "here's our single-vineyard pinot noir-to-be, the Jensen Mt. Harlan pinot noir. You're going to charge $55 a bottle for this stuff. How do we get from this" – I gestured at the purple stew below – "to that bottle? What do you do? And what would Davis do differently? What were they doing wrong when they called the pinot noir the heartbreak grape?"

Josh stared into the sky for a minute or so, mentally sorting his lists. Then he started checking them off:

"I've already told you quality has first of all to come from the vineyard – where to plant is the first crucial decision.

"First of all . . . Probably, when they were getting inferior wines, the grapes were planted in too hot an area. They got overripe and lost colour and character. Probably they were overcropped – the winemaker was taking five tons to the acre instead of two. And then, of course, they were paying no attention to soil. This is the most important. They weren't planting on limestone soil. Even in Burgundy, off the hill and out on the flats, they don't plant pinot noir, they plant gamay. It's going to make an ordinary wine down there anyway, so they plant gamay to have even more ordinary wine. It's the small differences in the soils between one parcel and another that explain the differences in the characters of the wines. So: plant vines in the right place, and keep their yields low. Those are the main things. Do all the others if you must: develop pruning and training techniques, irrigate properly, do canopy management, leaf removal, stress management by "deficit moisture," and the rest, but those are the important ones.

"And then what we do, keep the vineyard parcels separate, do batch pickings of early middle and late, and consolidate these later."

"So in fact you intervene all the time?"

"Yes, but not in the sense that Davis means it. We intervene to help the natural process. We're really lucky now. We can still make wine the way they did at the turn of the century, but with our technology we can detect problems early and take care of them when they arise. Look, there are a thousand decisions that have to be made on a wine along the process – up to the time it gets into the bottle. After that, there are really no decisions left, except for labels and glues.

"So a winemaker can be a hired gun, to help make all those decisions. Or the winemaker can make 500 of them and the owner make 500, or somewhere along that scale. The decisions range from the most minor – when to wash and scrub the floors, what type of bucket to put the wine in, moving the wine from one barrel to another – to, when do you sulphur the wine, how often do you test it for vinegar, what do you do if you get a vinegar bacteria growing in one barrel but not in another? And so on. How much sulphur? For how long? Do you filter? Are you going to bottle when it's 12 months old, 15 months old, 24 months old? Those are some of the decisions.

"Here's a simple example: at first, I kept the alcohol level of our wines around 12 per cent, because I didn't want them top heavy, clumsy – I wanted elegance. But in 1982 the Romanée-Conti people told me that pinot noir should have 13 degrees of alcohol. So I left the grapes to mature longer on the vine. That led to riper, richer grapes, and to the richness, structure and elegance of the great Burgundies." In 2006 that business of the alcohol levels was coming back to bite; it was a source of contention within the winery and part of the larger discussion in the wine world about what made a great wine. But I would have that discussion with Jensen later.

"I did all that," he was saying, "without burning the grapes, without what the French call *goût de brûlée*, a raisiny burnt flavour. This was a decision I had to make, not the winemaker. Typically, I participate in all the big decisions. Corneliu does absolutely all the day-to-day winemaking. But I have the final say. It's like wartime cabinet decisions. If there are 11 nays and 1 aye, and the aye is me, the ayes have it . . ."

I interrupted. "This, of course, means that first of all you have to know where you want to go, what kind of wine you want to make . . ."

"Of course, yes. The whole process of winemaking starts with a basic directive – what do you want the wine to taste like? You have a goal and you want to maintain that. Much of our intervening, a lot of the analysis Corneliu does, is to help protect this vision – to protect the wine from spoilage, or to verify a flavour, something as simple as when the grapes come in, how sweet are they, are they sweet enough? There's a lot of flavour development you can just taste, but if you can get an actual reading, so much the better."

"Okay," I said, "but come back to this matter of what you do to the grapes after they're in the winery, until they're in bottle. What are the decisions you must make?"

He resumed his mental list.

"First, what yeast will ferment your grapes? How do you stabilize the new wine afterwards? How long do you ferment and at what temperature? What do you do about the sediment, the lees? What do you do about acid and sugar content? You have to manage the cap that rises to the top of the fermentation. There are decisions about pressing. How long to let the wine settle? How long to keep in barrel? How, and whether, to get a secondary fermentation? How long to store and keep, and in what? Whether to remove the sediment. Whether to filter or fine. When to bottle. How long to keep in bottle? What to drink in the long, long, meantime? . . ." He grinned.

I leaned over to look into the fermentation vat. The grapes had settled some, but not much. The bunches at the bottom were being broken by the weight of fruit above them. The winery was making no effort to break them up.

"Doesn't look as if anything is going on in there," I said. "What in fact is happening, if anything?"

"At the moment, not very much. First thing in the morning, we'll add acid to the must . . ."

"I thought you didn't intervene?"

He looked impatient. "In California we virtually always add acid to our pinot noirs. Our climate is warmer than Burgundy, and we can almost always obtain full ripeness in the grapes every year. We can get our grapes at 24 per cent sugar, which is going to make a rich, potentially dark, full-bodied, full-flavoured strong wine. In Burgundy they can't always do that. There, the great years are the hot, dryer years, when the vines can get up to 24 per cent sugar, but many years it starts to rain September 1 and it rains all month and they have a big mess on their hands. They have to pick at 20 per cent sugar, or

21, or 19. So they are allowed to add sugar to the juice by a process called chaptalization.

"In California, it's just the opposite. We never have to add sugar – we couldn't anyway because it's illegal – but we don't have to in any case. We almost always add acid. The cheap way is citric acid, which doesn't cost very much, but you should never do that with good wines. First, because it gives the wine a citric flavour, and then because citric acid is not as stable. We add the acid that's the primary acid of grapes to begin with, tartaric, which is very expensive. About $250 for a hundred pound bag of it, and we add bags and bags and bags of it. But, you know, again . . . if you want to play with the big boys don't try to economize on the essentials."

"How do you know how much to add?"

"How much? That's part of what the winemaker does. We always add the acid within 24 hours of going into the fermentation tanks. We look at total acidity as well as pH, which are two ways of expressing acidity. When we get a low acid must that has a high pH, we add acid. In the lab Corneliu will see how many grams of acid per litre of juice he needs to bring the pH down to 3.4, or something like that. That calculation determines how many bags of tartaric we need to add."

Later, I asked Corneliu what the procedure was.

"We have to keep everything in balance," he said. "It's not so easy at Calera because we are using all the stems in the fermenter, and stems contain more potassium. Based on the history from previous years, we adjust the pH to 3.35, or down to 3, but when we add the tartaric it will adjust to somewhere around 3.7 when it precipitates out in the fermentation. So it will come out as 3.5, 3.26, which is what we want." The idea is to add the acid to the grapes, not the wine; the ideal is not to mess with a wine's chemistry.

Then, while the wine is fermenting, Corneliu will test constantly for the dropping sugar levels. Calera harvests its grapes really ripe, and as pinot noirs ripen they tend to lose acidity. Pinot noir is notorious for the pH readings going very high and the acidity dropping out as the fruit ripens. Or dropping out during fermentation.

So far it didn't seem very non-interventionist to me. In Burgundy they add sugar, in California they add acid. Would Jensen add sugar if he needed to? Assuming it was legal? He said he'd probably do some trials with it if the practice was ever legalized, as it is in Oregon. "My hunch is that it's not the key. Everybody wants to find the key to the Burgundian mystery, but I don't think that's it."

In the morning, we were drawn back to the big tub of grapes on the fermentation level. I peered in again. Still nothing much seemed to be happening. This was slightly misleading. Deep in the must, where the berries had been broken by the weight above them, yeast spores were beginning to feed on that 24 per cent sugar. They were just beginning the population explosion that in a few days would turn the vat into a seething mass of purple muck and foam. It's at this point that Josh Jensen and the other high-end pinot noir makers start to really part company with the California norm.

In all vineyards, in all grapes and in most bunches there are native airborne yeasts. When left entirely to itself, therefore, grape juice will naturally give a home to these yeasts. Alas, other airborne microorganisms are less desirable – for the winemaker, the vinegar bacterium is the most sinister. The California practice is not to take chances. They therefore sterilize the must by adding relatively massive doses of sulphur dioxide (though still generally below the human taste threshold) and "inoculating" the must with cultured yeasts later.

Some of these wonder yeasts are proprietary to the wineries that developed them, like the "Woodbridge," developed by the Mondavis, a low-foaming yeast suitable for barrel fermentations. Others were developed in France and in the labs of Germany, and include Montrachet, possibly the most popular, which is used for reds and whites; it tolerates sulphur dioxide better than most, but it doesn't work well with high-sugar grapes, and can be slow. Pasteur red, or French red, is a mixed population strain developed in the Bordeaux region; it tolerates heat and sulphur, and rarely sticks. Assmannshausen from Germany is used mostly for zinfandel and pinot noir, because it intensifies colour and imparts a spicy fragrance, but it's not suited for must with high solids, like Calera's.

Jensen is scornful of these products, and of American determination not to let nature takes its course. And although other high-end winemakers do use cultured yeasts, he refuses even to use the common term "wild yeasts" to describe the ones that come with the grapes. "Call them native yeasts, please," he said. "Americans are so apprehensive about using native yeasts they even call them wild." He calls the cultured yeasts "wash-day miracle yeasts."

"You kill everything with big doses of sulphur dioxide and then you put in a super miracle product you've bought at your super miracle chemist's supply shop using vinegar-resistant and vigorous but highly selected propagated yeasts to do a clean fast fermentation instead of using native yeasts. You're just not going to get the same quality."

Still, in addition to the acid, Calera does add a little of the natural sterilant, sulphur dioxide, to the grapes to try to inhibit "spoilage organisms" (aka vinegar) that might interfere with a clean fermentation. I remember Sara Steiner explaining that "yeasts are incredibly tough. They can take higher sulphur levels. They also metabolize a lot of that sulphur, so by the time fermentation is finished there might not be any sulphur left. So the sulphur inhibits deleterious bacteria initially, and allows the yeasts, when they come in, to make a clean fermentation."

For the next two days, nothing much seemed to be happening to the fermentation vat. No one seemed troubled by this. This passive phase can sometimes last four days before concerns are raised. No fermentation at all is very unusual. After all, pinot noir juice is an almost perfect fuel mixture for yeast. Crushed pinot noir grapes have been known to ferment overnight, and to get the most out of the grapes, winemakers must attempt to slow the fermentation down. This is one reason for the whole bunches: the yeast can't get at the sugar inside the berries, so the fermentation takes longer. This first-stage fermentation will produce an intensely dark, fruity, but soft juice. These berries will eventually be crushed by the weight of the juice, and the fermentation will proceed as normal.

Sometime in the third day, small foamy bubbles appeared on the surface of the must, the first sign that yeast cells were active below the surface. The vat began to give off the characteristic fermenting odours, a heady mix of carbon dioxide gases and grape aromatics. This is one of the most reassuring smells in the world to a winemaker; it's a sign that matters are proceeding as they should.

The vat also began giving off considerable heat as a fermentation by-product. Heat is a concern.

The Davis red-wine recipe calls for prolonged, cold fermentation. Cold fermentation is safe fermentation – yeasts begin to die at temperatures of 92°F and higher, and since fermentation can generate considerable heat, being "exothermic," musts can easily shoot up to 95°F. Then, as Jensen puts it, "You have a great big mess on your hands, a stuck fermentation, and you can't just toss in some yeast, because the yeast just won't propagate in an environment that has that amount of alcohol in it, so you have to then lead the stuff back into an active fermentation in another tank." Cold fermentation brings out the fruit in wines, while hot fermentation gives gutsiness, what Jensen calls "vinous qualities."

"Cold fermentation will give you fruit juice flavours – not soda pop, but fruit juice. Hot fermentation will give you wine characteristics, vinous flavours. So pinot noir should be fermented at a high temperature, as they do at Romanée-Conti. This is high-risk winemaking, but if you're going to attempt to scale the heights, to attain that ultimate last few percentage points of quality, you need to do it that way."

It's critical, therefore, to watch the temperature. Calera's stainless steel fermentation tanks, which range from 1,000 to 3,000 gallons capacity, are jacketed with a hollow outer casing in which cold water can be circulated to cool the must. As soon as the temperature gets up to 93 or 94, these "chillers" are turned on to knock it down. The danger point is usually thought to be around 89.

Jensen likes his fermentations at about 85, or 86 degrees. "It'll get up to 89, we'll knock it down to 82, 83, it'll go back up to 86. We like to have it up there near the red line. We're looking at it the whole time, and will turn the chillers on for an hour or two at a time. The main problem is they can spike up overnight. The sugar is the fuel in the fire here. By the time it gets down to 15, 16 per cent sugar the fermentation is really flying, and that's when there's plenty enough fuel to shoot the temperature up really high, so that's when you have to watch it closely. If the tank is 86 degrees and there's only 4 per cent sugar left there's not enough to push it up to the danger point."

One of the hazards of hot fermentation is increased risk of vinegar. "Vinegar bacteria are carried on fruit flies, and they're going to be in every tank of wine, and as careful as you are, you're going to see higher levels of acetic acid in warm-fermented wines. If all goes well, and it usually does, it's not that much higher."

I asked Josh why he didn't ferment in oak. Wasn't that the Burgundy tradition? It was, he said, but not any longer. Romanée-Conti uses all stainless steel now, and so do the other Burgundy houses that can afford it. "Stainless is the material of choice. For the two weeks that red wine is fermenting in a tank, you don't extract any flavour from the oak anyway, especially because most of the oak fermentation tanks are so old now that any oak character or flavour would have long disappeared. Basically, what you want for a fermenter is a neutral vessel."

A wine's character comes from soil and vine, wind and water, climate and weather, all controlled and shaped and governed by the winemaker's intentions. A container is just a container.

CHAPTER THIRTEEN

*In which grape juice transforms itself
into wine and the arcane subjects
of oak barrels and secondary
fermentations are discussed*

The red foam that appeared on the surface of the new wine was carbon dioxide gas. After a few days, when the must was fizzing, the gas pushed the suspended solids, the skins and stems, to the top of the tank. In a while this "cap" became quite thick, solid enough to stand on. Managing the cap is one of the primary tasks of the winemaker. But how – by "punching down," or by "pumping over"?

It may seem like a trivial decision, since either way the purpose is the uncomplicated one of keeping the cap moist. If it dries out, the skins could become infected with vinegar bacteria. And, if they're piled up on top of the juice you won't extract as much colour, flavour or tannin as you could. "Grape skins are where the colouring matter is," Jensen says, "And much more – the phenolics, the aromatics, the flavouring matter, all reside in the skin, not in the juice. But particularly colour. Colour is job one with pinot noir. So doing something with that cap is one way of getting a dark wine when the wine doesn't want to be dark."

So keep it moist. But how? The cap is a sort of giant teabag dunked in the juice; you can moisten it by using a circulating pump to shift wine from the bottom of the tank to the top, or you can plunge it deeper into the tank. The first is the Bordeaux way. It's rough, tears the skins of the grapes, and extracts a lot of tannin, but doesn't do much for colour. For cabernet and virtually all the other varieties, you have colour to spare, so you can risk it. But pinot noir hasn't enough resident colour. In Burgundy, therefore, the preferred method is to plunge the cap down into the juice, using a plank on a pole, or the human foot, which is perfectly adapted to the task.

Punching this cap down can be hard, even backbreaking work. The thing is *heavy*! But it must be done, at least twice a day as Calera does it, or six or seven times a day as other wineries prefer. Calera has come up with a technological solution, and has rigged up two mechanical rams with wooden plates at the end that slide along an I-beam just above the fermenters. They run on air pressure. One man can operate them, sliding them along the beam from one tank to the next. They can plunge the cap to the bottom of the tank.

The active fermentation takes a few days to start, and may be over in four days, a week, or longer. The Jensen 1987, the vintage of The Bottle, sat in its fermentation tank for 15 days before the stopcock at the base of the tank was opened. For the last three or four of those days, very little was happening, but Jensen likes to leave the skins in contact with the juice for a few extra days – the additional time increases fruit flavours, and the perfume. Other high-end producers of pinot noir do the same thing. Tim Mondavi, for example, sometimes leaves the juice in contact with skins as long as 28 days. At Saintsbury, they average 16 to 18 days.

It's a question of balance. The main influences on wine's flavour are the skins of the grapes, the yeasts used to ferment, the deposits of dead yeast cells after fermentation and how these are used, and the container used in making and storing the wine. The fermentation part of the process must get the best out of the tannins, colouring and flavour elements in the grape, and achieve a balance between tannin, fruit and acid.

Two weeks and a day after the grapes came down from the vineyard, they were fully fermented, the sugar levels down to vanishing point and the yeasts dead from lack of nourishment after their great binge ("belching carbon dioxide and farting alcohol" as a farm worker once put it when I was a kid). The stopcock at the base of the tank was opened and the new wine was allowed to drain through plastic hoses into a temporary storage tank one level below. This is called the free-run wine. The residue – the muck of grape skins, stalks, wilted leaves and dead yeast cells – was scraped through a hatchway at the base of the fermentation tank directly into the press, which had been wheeled over to receive it.

This press looked to me nothing like the old basket presses I'd been used to as a boy. Those rather more romantic old devices somewhat resembled oak barrels with half the staves missing, with an oaken plate that screwed down on the pomace, as the must-residue is now called, squeezing the remaining juice through the slats on the sides and down into a small gutter, whence it was led to barrel.

Calera's presses are probably their highest-tech devices. Gleaming stainless steel horizontal cylinders, they look rather more like smaller versions of milk-delivery tankers than anything to do with wine (or, it occurred to me later, like massive versions of those devices that keep mediocre food warm in steam trays at serve-yourself restaurants).

The white wines, the chardonnays and the viognier, which don't ferment with their skins, go directly from the vineyard into the larger press. The red, both the Central Coast pinot noirs and our single-vineyard pinot noir, are loaded through hatches in the top of the cylinder into the slightly smaller press, a sophisticated microchip-governed device that uses a soft membrane driven horizontally to squeeze the juice into a large tray below. This tray is on castors of its own, and has a drainage device attached to another food-grade hose, which leads to the same storage tank one level below. This juice is called the press wine, and it amalgamates with the free-run wine in the tank.

Because there are no grunting workers turning a massive screw, it's hard to see how strongly the membrane presses the pomace. The correct procedure is "light and slow." Few wine-makers now press too hard, on the theory that the press wine would become too tannic and astringent. Jensen agrees.

What happens to the pomace afterwards? On the farms where I grew up, the pressing would be even lighter than the modern practice. Then, in violation of all winemaking sense, the press-residue or pomace would be dumped into a clean tank, topped up with water, sugar and acid and a yeast culture added, and another batch of "wine" (which even these parsimonious farmers called "false wine") would be made. This was given to the workers later in lieu of reasonable wages. It was pretty dismaying stuff. Calera, in common with other wineries, used to dump the pomace. Now it goes into their compost heaps.

The free-run wine and press wine sat in its storage tank for only a few hours, just long enough to settle the grossest of the "gross lees," the sludgy sediment substantially made up of dead yeast cells. After that, it went into barrels as unfiltered, untreated new red wine.

The Davis red wine "recipe" would more typically leave the newly consolidated press and free-run wines in their tank for a week to settle the gross lees, and then filter and treat it, perhaps centrifuge it to clear it further and only then put it into barrels, almost clear, already pretty stable, and utterly without character, the enological equivalent of canned peas.

Josh Jensen, however, subscribes to the old-school Burgundian belief that at least some of the gross lees in the barrel will add body and dimension to the wine. "This is an absolutely horrifying concept to the sanitation-is-everything school of winemaking from UC Davis," he said, after the by-now-obligatory "I don't want to be a Davis-basher, but ..." He believes strongly that one reason the heartbreak grape is breaking fewer hearts is that Oregon and California producers of pinot noir are of like mind on many issues such as this one. "What distinguishes the good present from the bad old days is that many of us went back to the source, to Burgundy. We'd ask, well, how do they do it? How is the stuff supposed to be made? We weren't satisfied just saying, oh yeah, it's a red wine, I know how to make red wine ..."

After five hours in the holding tank, the wine flows

through more plastic hose to the level below, where the crew is waiting with newly cleaned barrels. The winemaker is also waiting, with clipboard and pencil and directions; each batch (the Early, the Middle and the Late) and each vineyard block, has been fermented separately and will be barrelled and labelled as such. For the white wines, the barrels will be filled only five-sixths, to allow room for continuing fermentation. The pinot noir barrels are filled almost to the top, the bungs inserted, the "labels" – small pieces of paper with identifiers scrawled on them ("10/25/90 Jensen Early") – stapled to the barrel fronts, and the barrels stacked in long rows, five tiers high, each barrel separated by small wooden chocks.

Filling the stacks, as arranging these serried ranks of barrels is called, is not as easy as it looks. Jensen, having tried it himself, is full of admiration for his cellar foreman, Abraham Corona. "The man's a near genius at lining up those barrels, five rows high, straight as an arrow, all by eye. In the days when I used to do it, my stacks never looked like Abraham's. Most people who do this use ten-foot-long levels; Sara bought one for Abraham but he just put it in the corner, and it's still there."

The wine stays in its barrel for 15 months. But it isn't entirely left alone.

This matter of the barrels is not as simple as you might think. Why barrels? Why this size? Why oak? Why, generally, French oak?

Premium wines, and wines for the long term, are almost always aged in barrel, usually 50- or 60-gallon oak barrels. Many premium white wines are also fermented in barrel, which seems to produce a wine with more depth, more dimensions to it, than those from stainless steel tanks; perhaps, as the wine breathes in air through the wood it takes on some of the aromas of the cellar.

Why 60 gallons seems the correct size, no one really knows. Perhaps it was trial and error over the centuries. Perhaps it was just a manageable size to stack. Perhaps that's how big the oak trees grew in the forests of Allier in central France. Perhaps, as Jensen suspects, 60 gallons leaches just the correct amount of flavour from the oak into the wine. Trial and error have shown that such a barrel seems to allow just enough oxygen to the right amount of wine to affect flavour positively, subtly and beneficially, softening the acids and tannins in the wine. Wine under gas in a stainless steel tank will never grow or develop, staying unchanged for years. Another advantage is the relatively short distance (about 2 1/2 feet) the sediment has to drop before the wine is clear. "Whatever the reason, 60 gallons seems to work. I don't know why. Maybe someone will find an 83-gallon size that works even better or 31 gallons, but 60 is what the French use and what great wine comes out of in France, so we use that. It's part of my method. Let's at least start with what the Burgundians do, and then branch off if we find something better. If it ain't broke in Burgundy, then don't fix it here. But if it is broke, if there's something you can do to make better wine, then start doing that."

The single-vineyard pinot noirs spend their 15 months in French oak barrels made to careful specification by a specific cooper in France who makes his barrels in a particular way out of wood from a designated forest. About a third of the wine will sit in barrels that are new. None of it will be in barrels more than four years old. The new barrels, particularly, will impart a warm and exotically perfumed flavour to the finished wine, a heady mix of vanilla, spices and a buttery richness.

Oak barrels are one of the reasons premium wines cost premium prices.

Calera's barrels are a mix of woods from the central French oak forests of Allier, Tronçais and Nevers. But Josh Jensen doesn't get into what he calls "hair splitting" on this matter of barrels. At least, not much: "We just buy sound barrels from a cooper with an impeccable reputation. It's very important that it be French oak, not American. Medium toast."

Not American oak? Medium toast? This is not hair splitting?

For producers with a finely tuned nose and a passionate demand for precision and nuance, it's really not. Many American winemakers are considerably fussier, specifying even the thickness of the staves, and the style of the hoops. And this business of French oak is not just old-world chauvinism: oak with a tight grain will release its desirable flavours more gradually. In general, oak from poor soil away from rivers is best – which is why the Nevers, Tronçais and Allier forests are so much in demand. The Limousin forests produce a looser grain, too strong for wine; so do the forests of Alsace. American oaks are also loose-grained and give wines a creamy taste, but are regarded as too strongly flavoured.

Still, if producers are not nitpickers, French coopers are hedged around with so much tradition as to seem positively fusty. The trees, for example, are split by hand along the grain, never sawn (so that the coarser oils are not released into the wine); the wood is then weather-dried (never, horrors, in a kiln) for somewhere between three and seven years. Then it's cut by hand into the 30 staves that will make up one barrel.

As a consequence, only about 20 per cent of an oak tree

is suitable for staves, and a hundred-year-old tree may only yield enough wood for two barrels.

The staves are bent into the barrel shape over a fire of oak chips and shavings – the coopers never use steam heat, or gas. It takes at least 40 minutes to do the job, and it needs precise handling not to let the fire become so hot that it chars the wood. Gradually the cellulose fibres in the wood break down and the vanillins and aromatics are fused into a kind of sweet caramel, glistening grey like the coat of a silver fox. It smells of new wood and bananas and cream, and every other kind of childish delight. This caramel, which will dissolve over a year or so into the wine the barrel will eventually contain, is described by winemakers as "toast." Winemakers can order their barrels with high, medium or low toast. Calera prefers medium.

Most of the Calera barrels were made in France by the largest family-owned cooper in the world, François Frères, of St.-Romain. The head of the firm, Jean François, spends much of his life in the forests searching for appropriate trees, and seasons the wood in the meadows above St.-Romain. The firm produces only about 75 barrels a day; his clients include the Domaine de la Romanée-Conti, the Hospices de Beaune, Henri Jayer, and the *négociant* Rousseau.

Each barrel costs better than $600 and Calera has about 1,000, Jensen calculates. "We get about 24, 25 cases to the barrel and we'll make about 25,000 cases this year, so that means we have about 1,000 barrels. We order about a quarter brand-new barrels every year, and sell them off after four years. This is a little like selling off a Cadillac after going round the block a couple of times, but it's a price of going first class."

If at this point Jensen and his winemaker did nothing further, several things might happen to the wine. It could gradually age and mature, as the polymers in the wine grew longer and more complex chains; the remaining yeast cells could finish their work and cease giving off a protective layer of carbon dioxide; the resulting contact with oxygen could irrevocably spoil the wine; the batch might start fermenting again, this time through bacterial action rather than through the life cycle of yeast; or it would do none of these things, which would be the worst outcome of all, since it would run the risk of fermenting in bottle, either popping the corks in the wine shop (leading the wine merchant to demand his money back) or tasting putrid and looking cloudy to the consumer, which would make a lot of wine drinkers very cross and put the winemaker out of business if it happened very often.

The winemaker has to intervene at this point, if only to make sure the wine is microbiologically stable.

Under the "Davis recipe" the solution seemed simple and obvious: stabilize the wines with relatively massive doses of sulphur dioxide, and filter it thoroughly through a mesh only a few microns wide, to rid the wine of any further hazards. This worked. Of course, it also removed much of the flavour and complexity, the life of the wine.

It's the presence of natural malic acids in the wine that makes it unstable and vulnerable to spoilage. The secondary fermentation sometimes happens spontaneously – in Europe, folklore says it's generated by some mysterious natural harmony, and starts with the rising of the sap in the vineyard. In more prosaic reality, it's the action of a bacterium, the leucanostoc, that metabolizes malic acid and converts it to the softer, and stable, lactic acid.

Calera not only doesn't try to prevent this malolactic fermentation, but actively encourages it. They want it. No, they demand it, and leave nothing to chance: if it doesn't occur naturally, they inoculate each batch with a bacterial culture that initiates it.

The reason Davis discouraged malolactic fermentation is, again, because it's high-risk winemaking: while it's going on, the wine is no longer protected from oxidation. On the one hand, it's no longer emitting a protective fizz of carbon dioxide gas, and on the other, the leucanostoc bacterium is very sensitive to sulphur, so the wine can't be protected by sulphuring. You must encourage a swift secondary fermentation, and bite your nails in the meantime.

Some wineries have isolated their own strain of bacterium. Calera purchases a number of different strains from a winery in Sonoma, each one known for a different property. "You just grow batches of it and transfer that to the wine."

Yes, but how much do you add?

Sara Steiner, to whom my question was addressed, said, "Oh, a small amount, a cup, maybe 200 millilitres, into each barrel. Maybe . . . we want to see a nice steady metabolism of the malic acid, but how much you need for, say, a 60-gallon barrel is not so simple a question. How many chains of bacteria do you need to do the job? Nobody really has an answer, it's hard to say. It's not nearly as simple a process as the primary fermentation. I can have all kinds of cultures in buckets, and they're growing beautifully, there are tons of chains of bacteria, but put them in a barrel and it just stops. I've taken to adding a small amount of nutrient to the wine to get them going. This is really a source of nitrogen for the yeasts that remain. Yeasts are very aggressive; they eat up all the nutrients and there's nothing left for the bacteria. So . . . feed the yeast and they'll leave something for the bacteria.

"You've got to go with what's tried and true and what works. There are good years and bad years, and different nutrient levels in the grapes. At Calera every barrel is its own little entity. The malolactic might happen anyway; I'm just reassuring myself that the ingredients for the malolactic are in place."

I asked Jensen why the malolactic fermentation was so important. He believes it's "absolutely a key to making great pinot noirs, as it is, in my opinion, a key to making great chardonnays. Malolactic fermentation for pinot noir was accepted earlier in this country than it was for the chardonnays. Even now, the majority of chardonnays, even in the mid-price range and up, are not malolactic chardonnays. For it's somewhat high risk, and the advantages of the chardonnay having gone through the malolactic are not universally recognized."

What does it do to the wine?

"At least three distinct things. First, it lowers the total acidity of the wine. This is neither good nor bad, just a fact. Malic acid is stronger than the lactic acid the wine ends up with, so the total acidity will always go down a bit.

"A second thing it does is add complexity to the wine. People often describe it as the buttery character, particularly in chardonnay. It adds an extra dimension, an extra subtlety to the wine and in my opinion what separates the great pinot noirs in the world, whether they are made in France, here or in Oregon, or New Zealand, from the everyday run of the mill ones is complexity. Not brute force, not powerhouse flavours, not silky smooth elegance, it's complexity, different layers of smell and taste. The malolactic, for a pinot noir, is essential if you are going to get all the complexity in that wine of which it's capable.

"And then finally the malolactic fermentation renders the wine microbiologically stable, therefore you don't have to filter it.

"So it's absolutely the key to making the wines in the philosophy that we want to make them, because if you can't get them to go through malolactic fermentation, you must filter. And then you get the second rate."

As soon as the malolactic fermentation is over, the wine is given a dose of sulphur dioxide, which in this case acts as an anti-oxidant.

To know when to do that is not so simple a matter either. The winemaker uses an instrument called a spectrophotometer and runs a series of enzymatic analyses to see how much, if any, malic acid is left in the wine. This has to be done, repeatedly, for every barrel, all thousand of them. Corneliu starts with composite batches, and only tests individual barrels if he finds something wrong in a larger batch. "We're looking for diminishing malic acid. You don't really care about the lactic. Presence of lactic isn't the issue. What you want is to eliminate the malic, get it so low that the wine is microbially stable. If you don't filter and you put the wine in the bottle, there's not enough malic acid in there for any residual bacteria to create any fermenting problems in your bottle."

Inoculant strains are tailored for various conditions, including high alcohol or low temperatures, which is Calera's prime problem. The barrel storage area is kept at around 55°F, perfect for storing wines, but malolactic fermentation demands at least 68°F, a huge difference. Only in 2005 was the problem essentially solved; the barrels undergoing secondary fermentation were placed on a kind of metal-grid mezzanine high up in the cellar, and surrounded by a series of hot water pipes.

I told Jensen that this inoculation business sounded suspiciously chemical to me, but he was indignant. "Not at all," he said. "We're protecting a perfectly natural process. We're just doing what we do all along, which is to shape events so the natural process can happen uneventfully." Later, he poured me a glass of his chardonnay and demanded I dip my nose into it. Obediently, I did so. "Take a small sip," he instructed, "and let it sit a moment on the palate." I did this too. "See!" he said triumphantly. "Is the difference not clear?"

The wine sat on the back of my tongue, smooth as glycerine. I let the aroma drift up into my nostrils. It was true – underlying the fruit was a faint, faint flavour of fresh farm butter, overlain with a hint of vanilla. I thought for some reason of my grandmother, perhaps because she used vanilla in her baking, and caught a quick mental snapshot of her arms, ropy with hard usage, up to the elbows in a tub of butter and flour, and I could smell the warm dairy acids from the barn behind the farmhouse. I admitted that if it was the lactic acid I was tasting, it was a thing to be admired. "See!" he said again, and pressed the cork back into the bottle, slapping it into place. "It's one more thing that makes better wines better."

CHAPTER FOURTEEN

*In which our wine makes its way from
barrel to bottle, and in which the
techniques of racking and fining
are discussed and dismissed*

For the next 12 to 14 months, the winemakers are essentially babysitting. Very little more is done to the wine except periodic topping up of the barrels to compensate for evaporation losses, and constant monitoring by the taste panel of Jensen, Dane and Vita to see that nothing untoward was happening.

The wine is not "racked" at all in this period.

This is another departure from standard practice. Racking is a simple method of getting rid of the dead-yeast sediment. The "clean" wine, wine whose sediment has largely settled, is gently pumped or siphoned into a new barrel. The sediment is then thrown away, and the original barrel cleaned and readied for reuse. Virtually all red wines are racked, and not just by Davis rules: it's a natural way of cleaning and beneficially aerating the wine. Unracked wines run a greater risk of spoilage, a risk, as Jensen puts it, that "some unwanted character and smells will creep in from the sediment, from the dead yeast."

So why does he resist racking?

"Yeah," he says, "it drives the professors to distraction. They look at that thick sludge in the barrel and they say, god, it's so dirty . . . you can't do that, it's backwards winemaking." But racking does something else to wine too: it diminishes colour, body and flavour. And since pinot noir is the "especially grape," it especially takes away colour, body and flavour from pinot noir wines. "If your goal is to make sound commercial wines, then the professors are right. It *is* risky. But if you're aiming to compete at the highest levels, and to get the wine into the bottle at its ultimate potential, you need to take those risks, because the wine can't afford to give up any colour, any flavour, any body or complexity."

In Calera's early years, the vintages of '78, '79 and '80, Jensen did three or four rackings through the production cycle. He stopped on the advice of Aubert de Villaine, who visited Calera in the early '80s, tasted the '81 vintage, and asked what had been done to it. He suggested less racking.

"We experimented immediately – half the current batch was racked, half not, and we consistently preferred the untracked wines. They had more colour and flavour and guts, more middle." With the '82s, Calera converted to a no-racking regimen. "And that's more or less where we are today. We belong to a small society called the Small Wine Producers Technical Society, with a lot of the pinot noir specialists as members, and in comparing notes, most of us have abandoned racking. Interestingly, Romanée-Conti doesn't even do the two rackings we still do, into the fining tank and into the bottling tank. They don't fine at all, but bottle directly from each barrel, barrel by barrel. Since they pick each vineyard in one pass they don't have to recombine the wine, and since they use only new barrels, they can get away with it."

He has no interest in following suit. Not just because of his batch pickings, or because he uses some new and some old barrels. "In tasting our wines, I seem to prefer the flavour of wine that's been lightly fined with egg whites. It gives it a little bit of elegance, and it certainly does make the wine clearer. If the time comes when we do fining trials of one vintage and we find that we like it better unfined and don't want to fine it, we won't do it."

By January 1 the tempo of cellar samplings starts to pick up. Each fermentation tank batch has spent better than a year in barrels as a separate wine batch. The winemakers do endless samplings, creating composites from the pickings and the vineyard blocks, tasting and retesting the prototypes. They go through several "every-barrel tastings" to see if they like the way the wine is taking shape. They check and recheck the sulphur dioxide levels. Some barrels may need a small dose of sulphur to help keep them fresh. The winemaker takes notes; the cellar workers move through the cellars adding the sulphur.

What they're tracking is development, the maturation, the chemical change of the wine. They're looking to see if anything "funny" is happening, anything off, that might be happening in the barrel. Of course, they're also looking for that occasional special barrel or set of barrels "that are just dynamite, really exceptional development. Those are ones you keep an eye on."

Steiner told me that "wines do interesting things. Some, for example, may age really quickly in a positive way – they're precocious. Others tend to be tight and it takes them a long time. You need to get to know the personalities of the wines. What is this vineyard like, what does that block do and how typical is this?"

In Josh Jensen's terms, this is called making friends with the wine.

Finally, the batches are amalgamated into the finished composite wines.

These amalgams make considerably more complex wines than any of the single batches. The amalgams allow the Calera crew to sift through the batches, choosing a base, a backbone, a fruit, a structure, the nose, the finish. "Josh will say, and it's true, that when you put the parts together you really do get something better than any one individual. I think the most exciting thing about a wine is what you can call complexity, and that tends to be lacking a lot of times in a lot of wines, and this is one way to get complexity, this careful control of the composites."

I asked Jensen at one point whether he'd ever thought of blending pinot noir with another grape, in whatever percentage? He looked horrified. "No. Absolutely not. Don't ever blend pinot noir. Not even 1 per cent."

By early May, after 15 months in barrel, the wine is almost ready for bottle. The composites, where they exist, have been tested and pronounced good, the few bad barrels eliminated. The samples drawn by the thief are clear, though not yet brilliant. The wine still needed to be "fined" – the last of its sedimentary particles removed.

Not, however, through the "Davis techniques" of centrifuging, ion exchange, cold stabilization, or filtration, all of which remove flavour as well as impurities. Not for the reds.

Josh does, on the other hand, lightly filter his white wines. He's unapologetic about this apparent double standard. "Whites are more fragile, they need more temperature control; they need filtration. We never even owned a filter until we started making chardonnay, and we still only have a little teeny plate-and-frame filter and a small lees filter. Wines with residual sugar or malic acid have to be sterile filtered – by sterile I mean you take everything out, including a lot of the flavour, but our wines, even our whites, have no sugar or malic acid in them, so we can do a very light filtration. We could bottle them without filtration, and there are some wineries that do, but I like the taste of the lightly filtered wines better. We do it to our taste. We'll do a lab trial of two or three different filterings, and pick the one that works best."

But the pinot noirs – never.

Or at least – not so far.

There's one condition that would demand filtration. Occasional vintages, in Burgundy and elsewhere, just won't clear by themselves, even with the help of fining agents, and have to be filtered. Although Jensen is braced for it to happen at Calera, he has yet to face it. No one knows why it happens, although winemaking lore is full of theories, including an old superstition that involves racking only on the waxing of the moon, which may or may not have something to do with air pressure and almost certainly has a lot to do with a kind of cheerfully gloomy superstition. "If we ever find ourselves in that situation we may need to do a very light filtration, as light as possible, but we haven't yet, thank God."

White wines have to be more meticulously fined than reds to achieve that happy state called "protein stability," without which the whites would turn cloudy when refrigerated, discombobulating the consumer and disconcerting the winery's cash flow. In Calera's case they're fined by dropping a cloud of fine clay called Betonies through the wine. The clay drags the sediment down with it as it sinks to the bottom.

Red wines are fined more gently. Calera uses the traditional Burgundian method, involving egg whites. These are vigorously stirred into the wine. Since the egg whites carry a positive electrical charge, they attract suspended colloidal particles, which are negatively charged, to form large molecules that are heavy enough to drop fairly rapidly through the liquid. The stirring has to be done with some dispatch because the electric charge disappears within a few minutes, and it's not as easy as it might sound – giving 600 gallons of liquid a vigorous stirring isn't as simple as stirring a sugar cube into a cup of tea. Six hundred gallons is *heavy*.

The number of egg whites needed varies from year to year and batch to batch, depending on the particulate matter suspended in the wine. Corneliu will conduct lab trials to find the minimum number that will do the trick. It can range from a low of one per 60 gallons to six.

All the Jensens are, finally, consolidated in one stainless steel tank – all three pickings, in those years when there are three, and both blocks. The wine sits on its finings for 17 days, and the clear wine is then carefully drawn off the top and put into the bottling tank.

And so to bottle.

For the bottle of Jensen 1987 that started all this, it was June 1989.

CHAPTER FIFTEEN

*In which the subtle matter of
quality is discussed and the
even more elusive matters of hype,
propaganda and fashion*

 So there it sat, our bottle of
CALERA
JENSEN
MT. HARLAN
PINOT NOIR, 1987,
along with about 11,000 of its fellows, boxed and loaded onto
pallets, carefully stacked on the uphill side of a yellow line
painted on the floor of the lowest level of the winery (that's the
arbitrary line imagined into being by the tax-happy state
bureaucrats; once the wine crosses that line it is deemed to have
left the winery and is immediately subject to tax, whether or
not it has been sold). Those cases of wine will wait there, storage space willing, until they are old enough to go out into the
world on their own.

Finished wine now, no longer grape juice.

Still a young thing, callow, not yet ready for a serious relationship with a real drinker.

Is it any good?

Will it get any better?

And who says so?

There are three or four ways of looking at it: the chemist's way, the connoisseur's way, the marketer's way, and the drinker's way. All of these intersect in complicated ways.

From the chemist's point of view, the wine is a complex liquid whose value is basically a synthesis of chemical flavours from the juice, skin, pulp and seeds of the grape, containing numerous compounds and elements, including: residual sugar (usually less than 0.2 per cent of non-fermentable pentoses such as xylose, ribose and arabinose – the glucose and fructose has been metabolized by the yeast bacteria); fixed acids such as malic (the predominant acid in apples), lactic and tartaric; various volatile acids; isoamyl alcohols; pigments (chemists support Josh's notion that pinot noir is shy on colour; under analysis through liquid chromatograph, nine pigments can be detected in cabernet, eight in zinfandel and four in pinot noir); considerable numbers of subtle phenolics, classes of "flavoids" that determine the minute differences between individual wines; trace minerals; and tannins. A chemist can parse a wine into ever smaller and more esoteric "VOCs," Volatile Organic Compounds. A couple of researchers at the University of British Columbia's Wine Research Centre, Canada's version of the school at Davis, suggest that "the most important are organic acids, proanthocyanidins (tannins), terpenoids (monoterpenoids, sesquiterpinoids and C13-norisoprenoids), and various precursors of aromatic aldehydes, esters and thiols . . . Glucose, fructose, malic acid and tartaric acid are stored in the vacuoles of mesocarp cells; proanthocyanidins and other polyphenolic compounds, terpenoids, esters and others are stored in the exocarp (skin) cells."

So there. That's what you're drinking.

Winemakers understand the utility of these chemical histograms of wine, and, despite their inherent distrust of the laboratory, generally approve of anything that enables them to understand their product better. They know, or believe, that chemists will never be able to make great wines in the lab, but it's reassuring to know that great wines actually exist, and not just in the minds of their makers or of the industry propagandists. It's also reassuring to know why something happens. For example, if you know that the phenolic compounds in the wine link together over time to form longer polymers, you'll more easily understand why a wine tastes and smells different when it gets older. In young wines there's an unresolved blend of acids, sugars, minerals, pigments, esters, aldehydes and tannins. It takes time for these elements to resolve themselves into a complex but congruent whole. When the polymers get too long, they drop out of suspension and the wine begins to deteriorate.

At the same time, the chemists don't know everything. While they're beginning to be able to build a three-D molecule of a typical great wine, there's still so much variation, and so many reasons for the variations, that the practical utility of such knowledge is limited. Winemakers still have to trust their intuition and experience; farmers still make better wines than chemists.

And these farmers still take things . . . personally. Josh

Jensen tells a story he once heard in Bordeaux, at a winemaking seminar, that neatly illustrates the philosophical differences.

The story tells of the proprietor of a great Bordeaux château (for the purposes of the story always unnamed). He was very wealthy, and all his equipment was first class. There was no better-equipped winery in all of France. All his senior executives drove Mercedes as they tooled down to the shippers to send their wines abroad. But the property never made wines that won wine competitions or were feted at the annual dinners of wine connoisseurs.

One day the proprietor instructed his managers to visit his neighbour, a farmer who had little money and whose winery was, to put it politely, rustic. On the other hand, his wines always received high ratings from wine lovers, and won competitions.

"We have to do whatever he does, so go and find out what it is," they were instructed.

The string of Mercedes duly set off and were greeted at the neighbouring château with politeness. The farmer was a simple man, but he understood perfectly what they wanted.

"Well," he said, "let me first ask you one question."

"Okay," they said, "what is it?"

And he asked, "Do you love your wines?"

"*What?*"

"Do you love your wines?" he asked again.

Since they didn't know how to answer the question, they got back into their Mercedes and returned to their own winery.

"Well, what did you learn?" their proprietor asked.

"Nothing," they said. "He doesn't have any secrets. There's nothing to learn."

Josh Jensen tells the story with relish, in the vocabulary

and rhythms of a parable. To him it contains a very large truth about wine. He's a man who really does love his wines. To him they are not just inanimate objects, numbers on a chart, figures for the bottom line, a calculus of cash. He loves them in a parental way; he worries that they are going to be all right; late at night, when the others have gone home, he'll sometimes get up and walk through the winery, laying a hand against the cool barrels, breathing in the heady, clean, fruity aroma of the cellars. In the burning months of the California summer he'll go down to the cellars late at night and open the doors, turning on the fans to let the cooler air caress the waiting wine.

Maynard Amerine, the eminent emeritus professor at Davis, the person who wrote or co-authored most of the standard English-language wine textbooks, told Josh, when he was starting out, to be wary of losing the scientifically detached air of the technician. Never talk about the personality, or the mood, of wine, the great man said, and since Josh was a young man and just starting, he took the advice to heart. Or he tried to, but it was no use. He did treat his wines with love and with wonder; he does, in that ugly anthropological word, "anthropomorphize" them; he does regard them as live beings.

He'll wonder about their mood, the mood of a certain batch of wine, or a barrel or two that doesn't seem up to par, or a batch that seems anxious and forward. Sometimes a batch, for no apparent reason, will get cranky, or weary, or will withhold its charms, or be shy. These are all terms Josh uses, and all phases he can recognize in his wines.

He even does the same thing for the vines up on his mountain. "The vines need to tell us who they are," he told me once. "And what wines they'll make."

At the large winery level, where wines are manufactured

as much as made, Professor Amerine's advice was probably sound. But Josh believes that believing in their personalities helps make it true – it's a part of why great wine does indeed have recognizable characteristics.

He soon discovered that no matter how much attention he gave each batch and each barrel, some always turned out better than others, and like any parent, it worried and delighted him. "Sure," he says, "it gives you sleepless nights. You worry more, whether you should do something to a wine, or withhold something. If you're emotionally involved it matters more, and decisions on when to pick, when to inoculate with the malolactic bug, when to bottle, become more personal. They are almost like your children, and if you have three barrels of wine that, because of the type of high-risk winemaking I feel we have to do, irrevocably spoil, they turn to complete vinegar, and we have to dump 'em down the drain or sell them to a distillery for a few cents a gallon, I mourn for them, I feel sick. You can say, well, you've got 1,000 barrels after all, but that's like saying, 'Well, you shouldn't worry if only three of your children die because you've got others.' I do worry and I take it hard. It's unrelated to the dollar loss. There is a dollar loss, yes, but I'm not emotional about that. I don't like it, it ticks me off, yes, but I'm not sick to death over it. I'm sick over the fact that those three barrels died."

What is the personality of his high-end wines, the Jensen, Reed, Mills, Selleck and Ryan? He had surely tasted enough of them to get a sense of how they differed.

He was, for Jensen, uncharacteristically reticent to pronounce judgment. Partly, he confessed, out of laziness and partly out of a belief that his job was to make the stuff and it was the job of the critics and consumers to judge them. There's also a sense that categoric judgments get in the way of enjoyment; it's a truism in the wine business that in the matter of taste everyone is right (with the accompanying suspicion that the wine writers' and critics' pronouncements are largely hyperbole, and, by giving the matter of tasting wine an air of profundity through the use of arcane language, they actually interfere with the enjoyment of wine by perfectly sensible and ordinary people). At first, he referred me to the descriptions in Oz Clarke's Book *The New Classic Wines*, which described his single-vineyard wines this way:

Jensen is the most open, with deliciously accessible flavours of strawberry and honey, sometimes developing an almost candied sweetness which ages to a thrilling combination of raspberry sauce richness, swished with the rasping perfume of leather. Reed has a less dense style – combining the savoury perfumes of roast coffee and earth with a fruit of blackberry and the herbal aromas of sassafras. Selleck is denser in every way. More tannic, slower to evolve, but magnificently perfumed, full of the classic Burgundian entangled mysteries of cherry and plum, wild raspberry, toast and cinnamon spice. The vines of the Mills vineyard were only planted in 1984, but already the wines are exhibiting that rarest and most haunting of perfumes – that of violets. Oz Clarke hadn't tasted the Ryan wines by the time he wrote this, but the critics are saying of it that it is perhaps the most subtle, and delicate, of all the wines offered.

I pushed Josh for his own version of this.

"Okay," he said, "but first let me say that I can't always pick them out in tastings, not even whether it's a Calera wine or not. I've tasted our wines at the Vintner's Club in San Francisco, and in recent years I'll usually like one wine a lot and it will turn out it's ours. In early years I'd go into the tasting looking for our wine, instead of just tasting, and it would get me all screwed up, so in the end I'd neither find our wine nor achieve a cogent analysis of the wines there."

He stopped, shook his head. "When I first started, I went to an important tasting at the top of the Bank of America building put on by Connoisseurs Guide. This was in the formative years of California pinot noir, and the '79 Selleck, a very fine wine of ours, was in it. The results were to be reported in their publication, which was quite important at that time. Now, when I taste wines I can have great days when I'm perceptive and accurate, and days when I'm off the wall. I know, as soon as I get into a tasting, what kind of day it will be. That day, I had one of those days. I ranked our '79 Selleck last. If I'd not been at that tasting, the '79 Selleck would have won, and put us on the map. Instead, it came in third because of my 12th place vote. I'll carry that guilt with me until my grave. It took us four more years to get to the top of the heap.

"After a while I learned to relax and resolved just to go in and find which wine I liked the best, which the worst, and which in between, and rank them, and since I started doing that, more often than not, I like ours.

"So, I don't think there's an attribute to each of the vineyards that will categorically identify each one. We go to great lengths when we're picking to bring the average of each vineyard in at the same ripeness and to age them in the exact same percentage of brand-new barrels. We try to make each element the same, so the consumer will never be able to say that a wine must be a Reed, say, because it was picked early.

"It's too early to tell with the Ryan, we've only had two vintages so far, but I must say it has the possibility of being a standout wine, very fine and delicate with plenty of nuance.

"The Mills has terrific structure but it often seems leaner than the other three. The vines are nine years younger. Compared to any other pinot noir from any other producer it is rich, full flavoured, dark and complex. But compared to our own vineyards it seems less rounded and supple and fat by comparison.

"The Reed most years has to me a sort of chocolaty, raisiny character. In personality it has acquired a softness and precociousness. It seems to get ready and say drink me before the others do. It almost always has the lightest colour. I've sometimes seen a brick-red colour right out of the press, although this is usually a sign of some age in a wine. Partly for that reason we now release it first of the single-vineyard wines. It's very smooth. Of course, the whole process of barrel aging of wine is one of smoothing and softening the wine, and that process continues in the bottle, but much more slowly. The trick in bottling is to capture the wine just at the perfect moment where it is still crisp but really lush.

"The Selleck is my personal favourite almost every vintage. It is also the fastest to evolve. For some reason, and we don't know why, it's always the Selleck that's the first to get clear in the barrels, the first to taste like wine in the barrels, the first to show its true quality and the first to taste good after it's been bottled. It seems to have one more layer, one more bit of depth and complexity than the others, and since that's what I appreciate the most it appeals to me the most. The Selleck is the most feminine of our wines, the most subtle. It seems to taste spicy, nutmeg, truffles and earth together, floral, so it is complete and complex.

"The Jensen is a complex wine and for me consistency of

complexity is really the ultimate compliment to a pinot noir. Pinot noir doesn't want to allow you to be consistent. When people tell me our wines are good I'm complimented, but when they say they are consistent, that for me is the jackpot. Every winery in California has one great pinot noir in it, and very often only one. To do it year after year, that's the challenge, the achievement. Also, the Jensen is usually the most tannic and also the leanest, the least rounded. It has some type of olive character, a spiciness, and ... well, the well runs dry after saying those things.

"I think between 5 and 20 years is when our wines show nicely. Sometimes wine writers who write about our estate pinot noirs say they are lighter-style wines to be drunk in a year or two. I think that's a misreading of these wines."

Like many people who drink wine for enjoyment rather than professional aggrandizement, I've always been put off by the rituals of wine tastings, with their arcane procedures and pretentious vocabulary; there's an inherent elitism in the world of fine wines that intimidates and drives away many a casual consumer. The world of the wine writer is one of magisterial authority; they have so much influence they begin to think they really matter, and they feel quite comfortable sneering at people who like a little residual sugar in their wines, or who like to drink a blush wine with fried chicken.

There is, in fact, more disdain expressed for the ordinary consumer in the wine business than in any other subculture, with the possible exception of haute couture. After all, the differences between wines, particularly if they are fine wines of the same kind, are so small, so personal, so fleeting, a quick splash of sensation on the palate, that learning can quite interfere with enjoyment. You don't need a PhD to appreciate wine; all you need is experience. The more you do it, the better you get, and the experience is best gained drinking wine with food, for enjoyment, and not in the swirl and sniff environment of what are essentially trade shows.

Many tastings are snob tastings, but not all is foolishness and hype. There are some real reasons for what tasters do, for the sniffing and slurping and spitting that goes on during these affairs. It's governed, to some degree at least, by the physiology of taste. The tongue is a clumsy instrument; it can tell only whether the wine is sweet (at the tip), or sour (at the sides), or bitter (at the back). The real seat of flavour and aroma in the wine are the esters and aldehydes, which rise as vapour from behind the palate into the nasal cavity. There they are dissolved and carried to the olfactory nerve centre in the brain, and thence to the temporal lobe, where memory resides. Memory is analyzed and judged in the higher lobes of the brain. The alcohol in the wine facilitates this process but will also very shortly upset the brain's equilibrium – which is why it is best not to swallow if you're tasting a number of wines. Eighty percent of the quality of the pleasure is in the smell, and the nose, therefore, is as important as the palate.

The consistency of expert reactions at blind tastings does indicate that evaluating wine is not all illusion. Generally, experienced tasters will agree on which wines are good and which are not. They might have different rankings for numbers one and two, according to their personal preferences, but they'll probably all agree on the top four.

This is how to taste a wine:

First, the colour. Splash a little wine into the glass, tilt it, and hold it against a white surface in good light. Check the opacity – is it clear or cloudy? Browning at the edges, and a light brick colour, is a sign of age; younger wines are deeper in colour. By tilting the glass and watching the wine seep down the sides, you can determine its concentration and viscosity, its "legs."

Next, the higher tones and perfumes. These are best smelled gently as your nose approaches the glass.

Go deeper into the glass and inhale slowly, looking for the deeper wood-and-fruit character of the wine. A wine low in acid will seem dull in the nose; high acid will seem sharp. American oak smells older; the French has a warm vanilla aroma.

Most experienced tasters will be able to evaluate a wine almost completely by this point.

Then take a small sip, letting it flow back into your mouth. From that, you'll learn something about the acid balance of the wine, whether it's tart or flat. If it's astringent, it will make your mouth pucker.

Take a bigger sip, place it behind your teeth and suck air through it, in violation of good table manners. That's the best way to give you a sense of flavour and body, of the weight of the wine, of how dense and complex it is. If the nose is dull but the flavour is full, the wine will probably develop. If the nose is rich but the flavour dull, it's probably past its prime.

Swallow the wine. Reflect on the residual flavours in your mouth. How long does it last? Does it feel clean and fresh? Or is it heavy, dead and flat? This "finish" is important – it probably contributes more of the pure pleasure of drinking wine than anything else.

The most difficult thing about tasting wine is describing it to others. The attributes are so elusive, and the standards for measuring them so abstract, that writers must perforce fall back on fanciful comparatives. (I thought back to the reading I'd done on pinot noir. My favourite descriptor, from a wine writer I generally admire, was "armpit," which she meant positively, if off-puttingly; and my favourite winemaker's reaction came when a writer described his wine as "smelling of eucalyptus," and he responded afterwards that he thought "eucalyptus smelled of cat-piss, but if they want to call it eucalyptus and sell my wine for me, let them go ahead.") The more common words used are butter, oak, toast, nuts, raspberries, citrus, coffee, black tea, tar, truffles, peaches, vanilla, yeast, cigar box, earth and eucalyptus. Wines are also described as spicy, prickly, tannic, full-bodied, honeyed, raw, burnt, bitter, youthful, closed, open, forward, reticent, alcoholic, mature, faded. There are also a few useful descriptors that are more technical in their intent. "Body," for example, means the heft of a wine, and is attributed to its alcoholic content; "finish" means the aftertaste – in great wine the flavour remains in the mouth for some time after tasting; "hard" describes a particularly tannic wine that needs years, sometimes decades, to mature; "supple" is its desirable opposite; "dumb" means wine not yet offering up its full quality, and is similar to "closed," which can also mean something similar to hard.

Sometime later, on my desk at home, I lined up bottles of Reed, Mills, Selleck and Jensen – again, this was before the Ryan wines were available. I pulled the cork from the Jensen and poured a little into a clean glass, tilting it against a sheet of white paper on the desk. It was brilliantly clear, with a deep ruby red colour. I sniffed. There were, indeed, hints of strawberry and honey-vanilla, with a faint undertone of what I took to be a kind of old-leather aroma. In the mouth, the wine was still tight, a little astringent – it needed another couple of years – but the strawberries changed to raspberry jam. Try as I might, I detected no hint of violets, the one word everyone uses about the wines they love best.

I pushed the unopened wines aside – keeping the Jensen to hand to keep memory fresh – and riffled through a pile of clippings on the desk, reviews of Calera wines from the professionals, to see what they had to say. The first one I found I couldn't identify, the name of the writer and newspaper had disappeared from the clipping. Whoever it was said something I thought apt about Calera Central Coast pinot noir: "A fine wine, an intelligent wine – perfect pinot noir fruit, with the flavour of the limestone vineyards, with good structure, perfect harmony, nuance and surprise." Apt, but wrong: the Central Coast pinot noirs aren't made from grapes grown on Calera's own limestone vineyards.

There were many others:

The *California Grapevine* said of the '87s that they were "medium to medium dark ruby colour; initially somewhat subdued aroma which opened quickly to show very attractive, rich cherry fruit with spicy ripe currant overtones with a note of vanilla; medium full body; assertive and moderately concentrated fruit flavours on the palate; well structured and balanced; moderate tannin; lingering aftertaste. Superior quality and highly recommended."

Robert Parker's *The Wine Advocate* liked Calera's Jensen the most – "The richest, darkest-collared, longest, most profound of Calera's offerings. It is also backward, very deeply concentrated, with multi-dimensional pinot noir flavours, and extraordinary presence and aromatic complexity." Wrote

Parker: "Since 1984 Josh Jensen has been producing pinot noirs that approach the aromatic complexity and flavour dimension of the best French red Burgundies, wines of extraordinary complexity that not only rival but also frequently surpass their French counterparts."

Joel Fleishman in *Vanity Fair* liked the Reed best: "Its nose of pungent, chewy black and red cherries leaps out of the glass, and in the mouth there's an explosion of clean, crisp, velvety black-cherry essences so rich and intense they make you gasp."

The judges at the International Wine Challenge, in London in 1991, said the Jensen "impressed tasters with its deliciously ripe, raspberryish flavour."

Chewy cherries and currants, along with a little raspberry, seemed the fruits of choice. I began to wonder what had happened to grapes.

There were dozens of other clippings, from Frank Prial in the *New York Times*, Alexis Bespaloff in *New York*, and many others – *Wine & Spirits*; the *Underground Wine Journal*; *The Wine Spectator*; *The Underground Wineletter*; *The Wall Street Journal*; Fleishman again; the *San Francisco Chronicle*; the *Connoisseurs Guide to California Wine*; the *Chicago Tribune*; *Wine Tidings* magazine (writer Tony Aspler liked the '83 Calera better than Chambolle-Musigny of the same year, and the Calera '82s better than the Romanée St. Vivant of that year); reports of the Vintners Club tastings of pinot noirs; the *Daily News*; *Wine Times* magazine; *Wine* magazine of London; *The New York Wine Cellar* . . . They all liked Calera, and they all liked the Jensen. So did Oz Clarke and most of the other new wine books.

Josh Jensen is wise enough to know that one of the reasons for his success as a winemaker has been because the wine critics like his wine; he understands the value of precise public relations – that an articulate tongue is as valuable to a winemaker as a fine palate. Influencing the influencers is important. In a country that is, still, wine-ignorant, if not hostile to wine, the people who write about wine are crucial; wine critics and the wine press are how retailers get to know what's going on, and a rave review can catapult a wine to the top. Other makers of California pinot noirs produce first-rate wines too, but many have never been reviewed, and their businesses are failing. Josh has warned his staff several times that there is no guarantee of continued coverage by the critics; they could decide on whim to ignore Calera. "Maybe they'll decide we've had our 15 minutes of fame," he says, "Maybe they'll think we're too big for our britches. I don't know. But we shouldn't expect this to go on."

In February 2006 I once again spent some time riffling through a towering pile of clippings and photocopies of writing about Calera, this time in Calera's sun-drenched office space. Many were copies of reviews I had already seen, though there were dozens of others. But after a while, I noticed something significant: the reviews continued until 1993, 1994 and then began to tail off. What reviews existed from later years were uniformly excellent, but there were far fewer, and by the late 1990s, Josh Jensen and Calera seemed to drop out of view.

What had happened?

Which brings us to the curious intersection of several ongoing trends.

The first of which is that 15-minutes-of-fame business Jensen had warned his staff about. After a while, established wineries in California, no matter that everyone agreed they were the standard-bearers, simply couldn't get any press. They could hardly get arrested, in Jensen's phrase. When he complained to a journalist friend of his that the wine press wasn't writing about established wineries, the scribe turned to him with a pitying look and said, "Josh, what are the first three letters of the word 'news'?"

"Oh!" said Jensen, the light going on. If you've been around for a while, you're not "news." In an environment in which wine was the new hot thing and California wineries were proliferating daily, novelty was naturally of the essence.

He could take some consolation from the fact that his wine had been received with admiration, even adulation, among a group of France's best producers, a notoriously tough audience. It happened in 2003. Josh for the first time joined the group of winemakers on what is jocularly called the Tour des Vignerons – a crowd of Burgundians and Bordelais and a sprinkling of Alsatians would gather in a different part of France each year, settle in a hotel, do a swing through the countryside on their bikes during the day, and settle in for some serious eating in the evening. The price of admission was to bring a bottle or two of your best wine. Josh took a magnum of the '87 Jensen, and to his relief it drank superbly.

"Remember that this is a noisy, opinionated group, everyone talking at once, you'd have five guys all telling bad jokes at once, all the rest laughing uproariously. As my magnum started down the table, you could hear the crowd getting quieter, and the whispering start . . . By the time it got to the end, there was silence . . . I think that was the greatest honour I have ever had, to be able to quiet down that crowd in that way . . . For days afterwards they would come up to me on the road, and congratulate me, they were still talking about this California wine that had made such a stir."

Nice? Of course it was nice. But it didn't help sell a single bottle.

"In a way," Jensen said, reverting to his didactic mode, "I've never felt, even at the start, that we've fully gotten our due. In the early years, you'd read things like, 'Chalone is the best but Calera is the second best,' or someone else was the best and Calera second best, and then when we vanquished that competitor, another would pop up. Then Oregon popped up, and Calera and California became the pretender, or Carneros, or New Zealand, the new flavour of the month, the new sexy young thing. For a while, Russian River was the sexy young thing. It's still in vogue but the newest young things now are the Santa Rita Hills and Santa Lucia Highlands. It's like a shooting gallery in an arcade, when you knock a target down, two new ones pop up."

It struck me that this flavour-of-the-month thing was exactly the reverse of what had happened when he first started Calera. Then, nothing was sexy, all was impossibility. Now, fashion dominates.

He groaned, a little theatrically. "Yeah," he said, "I sometimes think my kids will have had the worst of both worlds. While I'm here, they hear me moaning about getting no respect; when I'm gone, they'll likely have to put up with people asking them what it was like to have such a brilliant visionary as a father . . . More seriously, to develop an international reputation for making fine wines is not just a matter of a year or two. It takes decades. Burgundy has had a great publicity machine for two thousand years. Even Napa Valley was first touted by Robert Louis Stevenson; as far back as 1860 he was promoting its glamour and specialness."

Indeed, without tradition and track record, all you get is hype, fashion, celebrity. And the rise of the cult winery.

Which brings us to the second of the intersecting trends, the importance, nay, dominance, of a handful of American wine journalists.

There are a number of fine writers writing about wine – Frank Prial, Hugh Johnson, Alexis Bespaloff, Tony Aspler, Jancis Robinson, James Chatto, Oz Clarke. But the two men with the greatest influence on the business in America are Robert Parker and Marvin Shanken.

Parker was a government lawyer from Maryland with a strictly local audience when he took two gambles that propelled him to the top of the critical heap. The first was to take an early and categoric stand on the contentious matter of the '82 Bordeaux vintage, about which the wine press had up till then been divided – was it the greatest of the century, or were the wines overblown and overripe? Parker's public fight on this issue with the most-eminent-to-that-time wine writer, Robert Finigan, was a *succès de scandale*, and propelled Parker to superstardom. Parker said the '82s were sublime. His view prevailed, the Bordeaux producers clasped him to their grateful bosoms, and his newsletter, *The Wine Advocate*, became an instant critical success, as eagerly awaited and as feared as the *Guide Michelin* in the restaurant business. (It also reached 21,000 subscribers, at $30 each.) Finigan disappeared. Parker's second gamble was his early adoption of Oregon as the future home of the world's best pinot noirs (and, a few years later, to enhance his reputation as a man who feared no vested interest, his magisterial denunciation of the very same producers he had lauded earlier). The third thing that gave him influence was his invention of the 100-point scale for evaluating wines – the assigned number and the price made it easy for consumers to buy wines without having to wade through the admittedly overblown prose that accompanied his ratings. His invention is not without its detractors, although many others have now adopted it; some winemakers feel it creates an inappropriate atmosphere in which some wines win and some lose, and thereby lessens a broad appreciation for different wine styles.

In the course of an average week Parker will sip and spit his way through hundreds of bottles of wine (reds in the morning, whites in the afternoon). The judgments and ratings will make their way into his newsletter and, often, later be collected into a book. His judgments are always trenchant and frequently contrarian. A few years ago, when all of California and some British wine writers (including the great Hugh Johnson) were proclaiming (in Johnson's words) that "California challenges the world with . . . a growing number of luxury wines of brilliant quality," Parker was writing: "Much of the self-serving, overly exaggerated publicity about the greatness of California wines . . . is quite excessive and easily refutable . . . California has much to learn."

Marvin Shanken was a former investment banker turned publishing entrepreneur. His magazine, *The Wine Spectator*, is the lifestyle magazine of the wine industry, filled with gossip and anecdote, personality profiles, hype. It also contains a serious buyers' guide, and twice a year sponsors events called The Wine Experience, bi-coastal extravaganzas that bring together winemakers from America and Europe, critics and journalists, retailers and agents, and have become an essential part of the wine calendar in America. The most important journalist in the *Spectator* is James Laube, the magazine's chief taster.

There are good reasons for the hype industry, of course. There are 1,600 wineries in California alone – how is the consumer to judge one from the other? Never mind the floods coming in from Europe and the rest of the New World. A hapless wine drinker perforce has to rely on the critics to point the way, especially now that wine has overtaken beer as the biggest dollar-earning alcoholic beverage in America.

Many winemakers remain sceptical that the hype industry contributes very much to the health of the wine business. For one thing, critical judgments are made on the wines alone, regardless of whether they can be paired with food or, indeed, are much fun to drink. And Josh Jensen believes that the hype, and the resulting dependence on fashion and opinion, is destructive in another way. "Fashion has a huge role in the American wine business. I deplore it. It creates a pendulum of demand, encouraged by *The Wine Spectator*. The magazine will do a cover, say, that says gewürztraminer is now in and that's the variety of the year. Four or five years later they'll have a cover that says, gewürztraminer is now dead, nobody is ever going to drink it again. I think this is so stupid. It's like declaring bread out of fashion, or leg of lamb. That's idiocy. Gewürztraminer is always going to have a role in the wine drinker's menu, and if it's not for me personally a big role, I'll still drink it, and for some editor behind a desk to suddenly decide it's going out of fashion is ridiculous. It's a pernicious influence on the wine market. It makes it faddish, like couture fashion, takes it out of the mainstream, makes it elitist, not an everyday activity."

Comparative tastings are good for the winemakers whose wines win. And, in one famous case, was good for the American wine industry as a whole, and, by extension (because it effectively ended the French illusion that they had a monopoly on quality) for the world wine industry. That was the famous comparison of 12 American wines with the very best of the French at a blind tasting in Paris organized by a British wine merchant and publicist. The Paris Tasting, as it became known, upset the wine world by demonstrating without possibility of error that the Americans were no longer producing large and clumsy wines that couldn't compare with the best of the Old World.

But tastings, and the celebration of winners, and the creation of celebrity winemakers, and the self-celebration of important writers, have their drawbacks. If one wine wins, others perforce lose, and the notion of individual taste loses currency. Tasting conditions have nothing to do with the conditions under which the wines will presumably be drunk, which is at table, with food. The matching of wine with food can yield up something better than either wine or food alone. Which in turn leads to other critical traps, in which a critic will insist that one wine goes best with fresh malpeque oysters and another one altogether with blue points. And don't *ever* have oysters Rockefeller unless you have yet a third kind of wine on hand.

The third trend is the newly discovered sense of self-importance to be found surrounding the American wine industry. It's easy enough to track. Before the Paris tasting, few promoters of American wines existed, and those few who could be found tended to be either diffident or defensive, which gave their writings a shrill tone. The Paris tasting was salutary, and essentially gave rise to the phenomenon of the autonomous wine writer, beholden to no vested interest but the consumer. That in turn led to a dismissal of the whole notion of tradition. And then, by extension, to a transformation of the industry's own self-image from one of diffidence to one of confidence, and soon to one of arrogance. Suddenly, everywhere else but California (and, grudgingly, Oregon) was "Old Europe" – to use Donald Rumsfeld's useful insult.

Combined with a preference for the sexy young thing, this has led to the wine world's equivalent of the dot.com bubble, the phenomenon of cult wines and cult wineries.

A case in point is Napa Valley's Harlan Estate (this Harlan has nothing to do with Calera's Mt. Harlan; it is named after the winery's founder, Bill Harlan, a real estate developer). The "Harlan Estate Proprietary Red" from Oakville in Napa has only a few years under its belt, hardly any track record, no history and no evidence of longevity. It is a wine in the classic Bordeaux style, and from all accounts very nice – but people are trading it on e-Bay and elsewhere at 1000 per cent profit. Harlan himself professes to be amazed at its cult status, but his business plan plays to it; he sells his wine 18 months before it is released, and no one has even tasted it before its stocks are depleted and the prices go through the roof. And it plays also to the current fads and the idiosyncratic tastes of the two journalists most influential in American winemaking, James Laube, who calls it the "best cabernet in Napa," and Robert Parker, who has gone so far as to say "it might be the single most profound red wine in the world."

The winery suggests a price of $235 a bottle. But if you really want some, be prepared to pay a good deal more than that.

Another case is the Shafer Hillside Select Cabernet, which was listed at a mere $175 a bottle. The ubiquitous Robert Parker, in one of his 2002 newsletters, called it "a potentially perfect wine in the making. A skyscraper that builds in the mouth with multiple dimensions, amazing layers of flavour, great delicacy and tremendous purity. The prodigious cabernet sauvignon is about as good as cabernet can be." Of course, says the eminent British wine writer Michael Broadbent, "Parker is perfectly entitled to his opinions, though personally I can never reconcile expressions such as 'extremely concentrated' with 'great delicacy.' It sells in California for $175 a bottle. Bad luck on the British, who will have to make do with the far less costly 2001 Château Latour."

The fourth of the intersecting trends is the nature of the wines the industry was making in the early years of the century, wines Michael Broadbent calls "full-frontal, opaque, fruit-packed wines with an almost obscenely high alcoholic content," and that Josh Jensen called sledgehammer wines – fat, fruity, jammy wines impossible to drink with food. They're all better than 14 per cent alcohol. The Shafer is 14.9.

Broadbent blames the critics. Wine writers who want to be taken seriously will concentrate their attention on wines that stand out in comparative tastings, which means that assertiveness is a given. Critics generally prefer big wines; in the critical vocabulary, big means good, light means less good, serious means good, light and playful less good. These are not men of great good humour, and they take much of the pure fun out of drinking wine. Finesse is not a word that has much meaning to them; ponderousness is the prevailing style.

As Broadbent put it in the British wine magazine *Decanter*: "The influence of [these wines] with an almost obscenely high alcoholic content is, in my opinion, disastrous. It is now admitted – though not by all – that they are too heavy for food, too heady as a drink. The combination of a hot climate and later-picked riper grapes is some excuse. But where are the old and tried wines of yore? Wines of delicacy and finesse, with modest (indeed unremarked-upon) alcoholic content, wines to appeal unthrustingly to the senses? Wines perfect with food?"

The producers and propagators of these "full-frontal" wines generally deny they are merely responding to critical judgments. But I've seen unlikelier candidates blamed – even global warming. I asked Jensen about this.

"Global warming is a reality, every farmer knows that. In our business, we just know that we are getting to 24 per cent sugar earlier than we used to. Government bureaucrats and brain-dead Texans don't acknowledge it, but it is getting harder even for them, and farmers know it for sure. And one of the theories is that grapes have two kinds of ripeness – sugar ripeness and so-called phenolic ripeness. In a sense, the earlier high sugars means that the grapes haven't been on the stems long enough to develop all the necessary flavours that will make good wines; all they are is sweet. So, the argument goes, we have to allow for higher sugar still, in order to give the grapes time to come to phenolic ripeness. And since sugar translates into alcohol, that means higher-alcoholic wines are the result."

"Is this valid, do you think?"

He pondered this for a moment. "Last summer, 2005, I called a meeting of our staff," he said at last, "and asked them a what-if question. I pointed out that even our alcohol levels have been going up. We were around 13 per cent; now we're typically around 14 per cent, and we're among the restrained group. I said, what if this stuff about phenolic ripeness is just bullshit? Just group-think? What if it's just that critics, important journalists, just like high-alcohol wines, wines that are jammy, dark, fruit-driven? What if we are all just trying to win over those critics?

"I suggested that for the 2005 harvest we pull back a little. I said, I want to pick our grapes a little less ripe, maybe we've strayed from our traditional vision. There was a silence. You could have heard a pin drop. In the bubbles above their heads I could hear, 'Jesus, what is this guy thinking? What bloody nonsense . . . Where did he get this horrible idea, there goes our quality . . .' Well, we did pull back. We picked a little less ripe in the fall of 2005, and for the first time in our history we had to put hardly any tartaric acid in our wines. Well, you know what? I like our 2005 wines, they're very nice. They're not low in alcohol, they're at 13 per cent and change, but the quality is there.

"I mean, if even we were unconsciously responding to the tastes of Robert Parker and James Laube, think how much more responsive would be new wines with no track records?"

In 2005 Laube tasted some of Calera's 10- and 20-year-old pinot noirs. "He tasted them, and we never heard back. I eventually ran into him at a wine event and I asked him, Jim, how did you like our wines?

"And he said, 'Well, they're all dead.'

"'Really?'

"'No, they're dead.' He had insisted on a backup bottle of every one. So we had sent him 50 bottles that we can't replace.

We offered to go and pick up the second bottles afterwards, but he'd given them away."

Parker, for his part, is more even-handed. There's no doubting that his own taste is for bigger wines, but he does know the value of finesse. Still, for years in the late 1990s and early part of this century, he simply ignored Calera, except for one rather dismissive aside. Particularly after the 2001 bust, this hurt sales. Finally, he agreed in 2003 to do a substantial Calera tasting, and he was sent more than 60 bottles, dating back to 1987.

He loved the wines, he told the staff. They waited for his next newsletter, but nothing appeared. Months went by, nothing. A year – still nothing.

Finally Josh phoned him.

Well, he said, he was wrestling with the logistics of it – how to report on 65 different wines in a way that wouldn't fill a book?

Eventually, he published his verdict, though only on his website, not in his more famous newsletter.

Nevertheless, Calera can take some consolation: He headed his review, "California's Romanée-Conti": "I had the privilege, and for the most part enormous pleasure, of tasting through many of the single-vineyard Calera pinot noirs," he wrote. "Most of the vintages of the eighties were, and remain, spectacular. They are tributes to the extraordinary potential of these vineyards to produce world-class pinot noir. As in Burgundy, producing pinot noir is often a challenge, and sometimes the wines miss badly. Nevertheless, enough great wines emerged from the vertical tasting to convince anybody that Calera is one of the most compelling pinot noir specialists, of not only the New World but of Planet Earth. Credit must be extended to its visionary founder, proprietor Josh Jensen. Ironically, today Jensen rarely gets the acclaim that these wines merit."

"Did you notice that Planet Earth thing?" Josh said, grinning. I said I had. And so that night he brought a bottle of the Jensen '87 to dinner at the Tres Pinos. I hoped it wouldn't be dead.

It wasn't.

CHAPTER SIXTEEN

*In which the wines are priced,
distributors are found and the wines are
taken out into the world for their
final date with the consumer*

The final thing a winemaker can do for a wine is age it in the bottle at the winery for as long as possible – which means as long as he can afford – before putting it on the market. Calera's Central Coast pinot noir is usually sold soon after bottling. As a lesser wine, with fewer of the complicated chemical polymers, it doesn't benefit as much from additional time in the bottle as the single-vineyard wines do.

Nor does it undergo the process that unnerves winemakers and still baffles the chemists, the phenomenon called bottle shock or bottle sickness. The single-vineyard pinot noirs, like the great Burgundies, on the other hand, are susceptible.

When they're bottled, in the spring each year, the wines taste fresh and clean. "If you tasted the wine from the bottling tank you'd say, god, this is great. Then, six months later you open a bottle and you ask, what happened to this wine? Where did it go? Because it tastes . . . flat and insipid." Bottle shock turns wines simple. They lose all their complexity, become one-dimensional, boring. I've never heard any chemist's explanation for this, but it happens to all good wines. Pinot noir, being the especially wine, tends especially to get bottle shock. The six-month period is the nadir and then they start coming back, and once they've been in the bottle for about a year they're as good as they tasted on the bottling line, and perhaps starting to get better.

"It's a very scary process," Jensen acknowledges. "We certainly don't want our customers drinking the wines while they're in this state."

The wine, perhaps bruised and indignant as being shut up in a bottle, needs time to recover its dignity.

Fortunately, it will get it.

As they were bottled, all 970 cases of the 1997 Jensen Mt. Harlan pinot noir were stacked in the warehouse. But that didn't mean a customer could just walk in and buy a bottle, or a case, or a truckload. Nor did it mean that a restaurateur, hotelier, or retailer could order whatever he wanted. Good marketing calls for a strategy that includes control of supply, as well as shrewd pricing.

The first single-vineyard pinot noir vintage that Josh Jensen produced was tiny, one ton of grapes from 24 acres, or one twenty-fourth of a ton per acre, which yielded up just 60 cases of wine, almost small enough to put on the back of a pickup truck, which is how he delivered much of his wine in the early days. He developed a small route, through San

Bernardino down to Newport Beach, San Diego, and back along the coast, through central Los Angeles. He'd deliver the zinfandels and samples of his single-vineyard pinot noirs, persuading chefs and sommeliers and retailers to taste on the spot: his corkscrew was his busiest sales tool. Later, when he started making chardonnay, he'd do the same with it.

He sold his wine to his friends, family, friends of family and family of friends. He used what connections he could. He'd once met Ernest Gallo at a dinner at George Selleck's house, and as soon as he had something to sell he asked the great marketer if he'd taste Calera wines and perhaps recommend a few distributors. Although his production was only a few bottles, he'd already won a few medals and was optimistic Gallo would help. Surely the great man wouldn't feel jealous of a tiny winery? So he sent samples over to the Gallo winery. Several weeks went by, and he heard nothing. He phoned, with no result. He phoned again. After several months of this, a short, terse letter arrived. "I see no future for any of your wines," Gallo wrote, "You should feel free to approach my distributors on your own, since I cannot recommend your wines to them."

Settling on the price is a key decision for a winemaker; proper pricing can determine the success of his business. Josh does the final pricing at the last possible minute, and sifts the prices as little as he can.

The single-vineyard wines were priced at $18 for the '78 vintage, which was sold entirely in half-bottles in 1981, with a limit of three half-bottles per customer. The $18 price held for four years. The '82s, which Jensen felt was his best wine to that time, went up a notch to $23 for the Jensen and Reed and $25 for the Selleck. They stayed at that level for another three or four years, and then went up to the $30 level. In the early '90s his wines, like all other California wines, started to get more expensive. By 1999 the single-vineyard pinot noirs were retailing at $80 a bottle, and were selling out each year.

After the lamentable 2001 year, sales evaporated. Not just Jensen's – everywhere. He was forced to cut back sharply, to the $50 range. They've been there ever since.

"When we came out with our first vintage of pinot noir I set the price deliberately high, at $18 a bottle. In a way the price didn't matter, only the idea of the price level did. There'd been some word of mouth about the wines, which helped, and it was such a tiny quantity, really, that we could have priced it anywhere we wanted. It wasn't going to make a whole lot of difference to our cash flow. It almost didn't matter in terms of cash or profit. But $18 was higher than almost anybody was pricing similar wines at that point, so it seemed like a good number to go in with, to stake a claim, to assert something about our product. People said to me, why don't you price it at $7.50 now, and go up to $18 later, but I didn't want to get customers used to paying $7.50, because they'd be ticked off when we raised the price to $18. We do get people saying our wines are too expensive, but at least they can't say, I used to buy it for $7.50 and now it's $35 and that's five times the price and that's a rip-off.

"I never thought in my wildest dreams that our wines would be priced at $30 or $35, but I did think they'd get up to $25, or some such. So I didn't want to start low and travel all that distance."

How are prices set?

"It's quite subjective, a lot of it. I look at three things. First is the quality of the wine we're pricing relative to the competition, other American pinot noirs as well as Burgundies. Secondly, I look at where we've been in pricing and how long we've been there. Thirdly I factor in where we want to be in terms of a long-term pricing strategy. In other words, do we eventually want to get our wine to be $300 a bottle? No, I don't think so. But we're pretty much a price leader for American pinot noir. There are a couple of wines at our level and there are a couple just above us. We'll watch this closely. I don't want to be too aggressive in getting out in front of the competition."

Pricing, therefore, is based partly on availability (yield), partly on demand, partly on what the competition is charging for similar wines and partly on a long-term strategy. "You figure out what it costs you to grow it and make it and what it costs you to live, and that's what the wine should cost. You don't raise your prices just because you know you can get it. You don't want to alienate your customers, because your old customers got you where you're at."

The release date, as the wines coming onto market is called, will differ each year depending on the yield and the character of the wines – hard, closed wines should be kept in the winery longer, and one year might be released after the following vintage because of it.

Each vineyard's wines will he shipped at different times, starting in the spring. As they sit in the warehouse, Josh formulates plans for release. For example, he could put the Reed out in February, the Jensen in May, the Mills in September and the Selleck the following February. The timing would depend on the market. Four different releases a year would probably overstrain the market, and would lessen the chances of each wine getting reviewed; on the other hand, releasing them all at once would get them reviewed, but only once.

Even for the established wineries these reviews are important. Many retailers take the reviewers' judgments seriously, and base their orders accordingly.

In the winter of 2005–6 he released nine new wines and three "library selections" – what in the book trade would be called backlist wines. The single-vineyard pinot noirs were all from the 2001 vintage. Selleck was the most expensive, at $55 a bottle; the Jensen was $50, the Reed $50 and the Mills $40. Other releases were the 2002 Central Coast chardonnay, at $14 a bottle, the 2002 Central Coast pinot noir at $22, the 2001 El Niño California chardonnay at $10.50, the 2000 Mt. Harlan chardonnay at $34, and (an experiment) a dessert viognier in half-bottles of $26. Library wines released were 1995 Mt. Harlan chardonnays at $49, 1995 Mills pinot noir at $55, and 2002 viognier at $36. You could also buy a Mt. Harlan sampler pack, six half-bottles for $110, which included the 2003 pinot noir from the "new baby," Ryan.

In the first few years, while he was still selling his wine door-to-door in a station wagon, Josh developed his mail-order business. His first customers were everyone he knew, his family, and everyone his family knew. It has been amplified and purged many times since then, but his mail-order customers are still the first to get access to each vintage. Partly out of loyalty, and partly because they are the most profitable sales for the winery.

He may be a man who markets on intuition, but he has developed a marketing system that is straight MBA, and is designed to maximize sales across the production board.

Clients are divided into three categories.

The first is the mailing list customer, individuals who order directly from the winery. They account for 5 per cent of the volume and 10 per cent of the winery's revenue.

The second is the wholesaler. For the first ten years Jensen spent most of his energy building a national reputation and a national distribution network. As a result, his wines are available in 42 of the 50 American states. Calera has wholesale distributors in most major U.S. markets except Atlanta, and these wholesalers account for 85 per cent of Calera's business. About 40 per cent of the product is sold in California. The other big markets are New York/New Jersey, Chicago, Washington DC, Baltimore, Texas and Florida.

The third category is the export market, a little more than 10 per cent of the total. Japan is by far the biggest customer (Calera is virtually a cult wine in Japan) followed by Britain and 13 other countries from Denmark to Hong Kong. You can buy Calera wines in nine of the ten Canadian provinces. In those markets where the only "customer" is a large state bureaucracy, like Ontario, Calera has a commission agent in place.

In the 1990s, when his wines were red-hot in the marketplace, he developed what was essentially a rationing system for the single-vineyard wines. Except for individual mail orders, customers were required to buy a certain quantity of the workhorse wines, the Central Coast chardonnays and pinot noirs, before being given access to the single-vineyard pinot noirs, the Mt. Harlan chardonnay or the viognier. Jensen put it the other way around, arguing that customers were "rewarded" with a quota of single-vineyard pinot noirs in the proportion that they bought the Central Coast wines. So if a large wholesaler bought 2 per cent of the total production of the Central Coast wines one year, he got allocated 2 per cent of the premium wines the next.

After 2001 the system was abandoned as unworkable. It was hard enough to sell any wine from 2001 to 2004, and customers would no longer tolerate complicated allocations.

Old system or new, part of the problem is inventory control, and that depends on yield. The large wholesalers are the core of his business, and he needs to keep them happy. He needs to have enough Selleck and Jensen and Reed and Mills and chardonnay to offer them in amounts in which they don't feel they're getting short-changed. If he sold all the Jensen to his mailing list, the distributors would lose interest, even in good years. It would be profitable in the short term, but suicide in the long term, because he's dependent on his distributor network.

Jensen is a strong proponent of exporting. He'd like his exports to be as much as 20 per cent of sales. He wants his wines available as widely as possible, on the grounds that his reputation can only be enhanced by a presence in overseas markets. Also, it's a hedge: the American wine market fluctuates wildly, and he doesn't want all his eggs in one national basket – America, after all, was a country that not too long ago outlawed wine altogether.

Through the 1980s England accounted for 80 per cent of Calera's exports. It wasn't hard to figure out why – a sophisticated clientele existed in a country that produces virtually no wine, so for at least a century England has been the freest of the world's wine markets. The French don't drink Italian wines, and the Italians don't drink German wines, but the English are willing to consider wines from all countries.

In 1992, for the first time, Japan edged out England as

his biggest market; Japan has remained his best customer ever since.

Writing in his own wry style in one of his newsletters, Jensen described the export business:

"*Sometimes we get labelling, invoicing or documentation instructions from our importer that conflict with the instructions from his government. In the worst cases, both these sets of instructions will conflict not only with each other but also with orders issued by a sort of super government, the EC.*

"*Then what do you do? Our fearless office staff just forges ahead, letting no obstacle block their path to Export Heaven. But I'd be less than candid if I implied that they share my love of exporting. The paperwork is just mind-boggling. We now have about 5,000 different importer's strip labels in our arsenal, but we never seem to have the right one. And we are often asked to remove the U.S. government-required health warning labels. Most other countries think these things are a real joke. What's more, for the EC we have to white out the words "Contains sulphites," so beloved of our own government. Those words are illegal in the EC.*

"*One way I'll try to motivate my staff so they'll complete the blizzard of paperwork is to read them lengthy quotes from overseas publications that write about Calera. Those written in English I can handle. French too. I also pretend I can translate all the others. German, Swedish, Italian, no problem. Estonian, Turkish, Hungarian, Hindi, you name it, I'll give them the gist of the article. Often these translations include very specific and praiseworthy mention of the excellence of the Calera forms, shipping documents, paperwork and special labelling. Our happy staff is constantly amazed that wine writers in these far-off countries know the names of individual Calera employees and single them out for the accuracy, elegance and clarity of their work . . .*"

Sometimes, marketing has peculiar national hazards, and commenting on these can be occasionally . . . counter-productive. Here's Josh on one of the state liquor boards, the Liquor Control Board of Ontario:

"Sometimes your actual customer, when exporting, is a government. Good god! Canada is a capitalist, free market country, right? Well, it turns out that if you're going to export to Canada, the people on the other end doing the buying aren't really people at all, but government bureaucrats! The Liquor Control Board of Ontario is the worst. They try to place the craziest orders, and then typically take two or three months beyond the due date on the invoice to pay you. A few years ago they did a lab test on one of our wines, and decided something was wrong with the wine. They destroyed the entire ten-case shipment (or said they did) without notifying us. We only learned about it six months later when we were making our 50th attempt to get them to pay. Needless to say, they never paid. What are you going to do, sue them? In their own courts? And why do we put up with this kind of tomfoolery? Because Toronto, the capital of the Province of Ontario, is the biggest city and the most important wine market in Canada. And Canada, as a country, is the largest export market for American wines."

Then, by the time he wrote his mailer the following summer, he had discovered another important fact about the LCBO:

"ERRATA

"I'd like to correct a typographical error that somehow appeared in our last brochure, concerning the Liquor Control Board of Ontario, Canada (LCBO). I really don't know how such a thing could have occurred, probably due to my having gotten so 'care-worn' and 'weather-beaten' over the years, but apparently our brochure described a previous unhappy experience with the LCBO

and may or may not have included the words, *The LCBO is the worst.*

"As luck would have it, shortly after we mailed out that brochure, our agent in Ontario, a solid, hard-working wine guy, got one of the biggest orders we've ever had, for 329 cases of wine, from the LCBO. That was when the comments allegedly contained in our brochure were brought to the attention of the highly respected Board members and the many fine, upstanding, diligent employees of the LCBO. They called our agent in on the carpet and, as we say out here in the west, worked him over pretty good. The alleged comments that may or may not have been printed in our mailer – almost certainly by typographical error, if in fact they were printed – damn near queered this giant order.

"If it was I who wrote the ill-considered passage that may or may not actually have been printed in our brochure – and we (note the use of we all of a sudden) are neither confirming nor denying that we ever wrote such a thing – it was not at all intellectual on our part. If I wrote it, I was probably the victim of being too 'confident' of the accuracy of my own position on the matter.

"Be that as it may, I want to go on record as saying that in placing that one order the LCBO became ONE OF THE BEST, and when they paid us in full and on time the brilliant visionaries who make up the LCBO, and their many loyal, hard-working employees – and in fact all the beautiful, congenial and far-sighted residents of the entire Province of Ontario – immediately became THE BEST."

The following day I went to visit Jensen at his booth at the California Wine Experience, at San Francisco's Marriott hotel. It cost me $100 just to get into the tastings. The hotel ballroom was jammed to the point of unpleasantness.

Jensen was pouring his Central Coast pinot noir and chatting to customers. I saw Ernest Gallo sniffing a glass, Francis Ford Coppola holding forth to a slightly awestruck crowd. (Wine people can be snobs, but they know a star when they see one; some of them had probably sat through his lecture earlier in the day: "Winemaking and Filmmaking: A Parallel Experience.") Some of the Mondavis were there. So was Joy Sterling and her father Barry. And winemakers and proprietors from 145 other premium wineries in the state.

The Grand Tastings, as they were described, took place in one of the ballrooms of the Marriott. For my $100 I got a tasting book, with the labels and descriptions of all the participating wineries, and as many glasses for tasting as I needed. The wineries were in four aisles, and off to the right was a food area, cheeses, pâtés and terrines, bowls of fruit. For another couple of hundred I could have attended other lectures, a breakfast talk by Marvin Shanken, a lecture on wine and your health (a bow to Josh's eco-terrorists), a talk by Oz Clarke of the *London Daily Telegraph* on the New Classic Wines (by no coincidence at all the title of his recent book – why else would he have flown in from Britain for a 36-hour stay?).

I asked Josh later how important these shows were.

"Absolutely necessary to be there," was his response.

Because a scary proportion of small California wineries operate on the edge of bankruptcy, much depends on public acceptance, and therefore public relations, and promotion. As Lee Stewart, owner of the former Souverain winery, once put it, "Any jackass can make wine, but it takes a super jackass to market it."

Even the name, Calera, was chosen with an eye on the markets.

"I think we looked at about a thousand names before deciding on Calera. It has a nice resonance with limestone, which as you know, I think critical for good pinot noir. And it's pretty-sounding and easily pronounced in most languages."

Labels, too, are an important part of the image. Jensen asked Jim Robertson, whose design and bookmaking firm in Covelo, California, is called Yolla Bolly Press, to design his labels.

"For me, the classic wine label is Château Latour, which has only seven words on it." (I looked this up later. The label reads, *Grand-vin du château Latour, 1967, Appellation Pauillac Controlée, Mis en bouteilles en château*, a total of 13 words, but you see what he means − Latour's is not a label to run on endlessly about whether it goes better with fish or fowl, or to wax eloquent about the vinification techniques or the *terroir*.) "I'm a Burgundian, but as far as labelling is concerned I like the style of those grand Bordeaux châteaux. They simply say, Here I am, take it or leave it. So I tried to emulate that." In the Burgundian fashion, Jensen wanted his labels to show the vine-yard name bigger than the company name. "At first, Jim just couldn't see that. So I sent him some (empty) bottles of Burgundy, and then he saw how the domaine name was always prominent, and then he got it."

So the early labels said:

Calera
JENSEN
1989
California pinot noir
Table wine

Produced & bottled
by Calera Wine Company
Hollister, California

The word "Jensen" was the largest on the label, but at first people didn't know what it was. So they asked for Calera wines, and got into that puzzled tangle with the winery: which Calera? The Calera pinot noir. Which Calera pinot noir? The Calera one . . .

The next iteration dropped the word California, added Mt. Harlan, and added the word "vineyard" after Jensen as an aid to stumped consumers. They also added the word "grown." So the labels read:

CALERA
JENSEN vineyard
Mt. Harlan pinot noir
1989
Grown, produced & bottled
by Calera Wine Company
Hollister California
Table Wine

The table wine line, under California law, designated a wine that is 12.5 per cent alcohol with a 1.5 per cent margin on either side. It is taxed less than a wine of say 14 per cent and more than a wine of less than 11 per cent.

In 2005 the labels were changed again, and simplified even more. My bottle of 2003 Ryan read as follows:

Calera
2003
Ryan
Vineyard
Pinot noir
Mt. Harlan.

Just eight words, even fewer than Château Latour's.

But it's on the back labels that Calera really parts company with other wineries. Most simply use their back labels for meaningless propaganda, sometimes amusing but almost always useless. Here, for example, is the Aussie phenomenon Yellowtail on its back label: "On sweeping alluvial plains formed by the great Murray River basin, nature's sun-drenched vineyards and leaping kangaroos perfectly co-exist in this wondrous habitat . . . The Shiraz bounds forward from the glass with berry and vanilla oak aromas. Subdued earth tones with soft ripe sweetness and displayed in perfect harmony with fine tannins . . . Perfect with steaks, pastas and even kangaroo fillets."

Others do rather better. The Marlborough New Zealand estate called Spy Valley, which produces one of my favourite sauvignon blancs, lists the harvest date, the Brix at harvest, the pH, and the alcohol level, and even their propaganda paragraph was more informative: "After gentle pressing all parcels were fermented in stainless steel tanks. Near the end of fermentation the wines were transferred and aged on fine lees until bottling . . ." Then they give up and yielded to hype: "The wine exhibits pungent tropical fruit aromas and a subtle herbal note . . . with classy fruit acidity."

Calera's new back labels take another tack altogether. They are probably the most informative in the trade, without any of the hype and "perfect with fish" tripe of so many others. For example, the Ryan vineyard back label shows, on its left-hand-side, a small map of the vineyards. Above the map it says: "The wine in this bottle is exclusively from pinot noir grapes grown in Calera's 13.1 acre Ryan Vineyard in 2003." Below the map, the housekeeping stuff, phone, website and address. The mind-boggling detail is on the right:

American Viticultural Area (AVA): Mt. Harlan

Mountain Range: Gavilan Mountain

County: San Benito

Region: California's Central Coast

Predominant geology: Limestone

Average elevation: 2,400 feet above sea level

Vineyard location: 9 miles south of Hollister, 90 miles south of San Francisco, 25 miles east (inland) of Monterey / Carmel

Owned by: Calera Wine Company

Number of vines: 14,596 (100% pinot noir)

Vine spacing: 7.5 x 4.5, 7.5 x 5, and 8 x 4.5 (feet)

Vines per acre: 1,278

Exposure of slope: West / Southwest

Year planted: 1998 (9.4 acres) & 2001 (3.7 acres)

Rootstock: 110R, 5C and 1103 Paulsen

2-year average crop yield (2002 through 2003): 0.58 tons per acre (8.7 hectolitres of wine per hectare of vineyard)

2003 Ryan Harvest Data

Dates of harvest: October 2–7

Tons harvested: 12.3

Tons per acre: 0.94

Average ripeness: 25.1% sugar

2003 Ryan Winemaking Data
Fermentation: Native yeasts
Barrel aging: 16 months in 60-gallon French barrels (30% new)
Malolactic fermentation: 100%
Filtration: None
pH: 3.79
Date of bottling: March 1 2005
Quantities bottled:
    8580 bottles (750 ml)
    1080 half-bottles (375 ml)
    42 magnums
    6 jeroboams
    = 769 full case (12 x 750 ml) equivalents.

    Plus of course, the usual nanny-state warnings from the government of California . . .

"The rest of the packaging is important too," Jensen told me, as he poured a glass of pinot noir for a thirsty seeker after truth at the Marriott. "It's all part of the wine's image and positioning. The labels we've discussed. But even the bottles. I'm using imported French bottles for my premium wines. If you're going to charge $50 a bottle for your product, it should be properly packaged, and the French bottles have an opulent look. I buy corks of the right length, with the winery name and the date stamped on them. And, until recently, classic lead-foil caps, red for the reds, silver for the whites." He motioned to the foil cap he'd just stripped from another bottle of Central Coast. "They've now banned lead in California, although they've been using it in Europe for centuries without hazard, they're convinced here that it'll poison everyone."

I moved out into the crowded ballroom. The room was abuzz with conversation, punctuated by the peculiar gurgle-gargle and ringing spits of the wine world. Otherwise the atmosphere was the same as any other trade show, a mix of enforced jollity, anxiety, weariness and deal-making. I tasted a few pretty ordinary wines, but was suddenly thrilled with an Acacia pinot noir, from their St. Clair vineyard in Carneros, an extraordinary complex of fruit and oak that jolted me into remembering why I was there. Apart from being briefly side-tracked by a wonderful sangiovese from Atlas Peak Vineyards, a small Napa winery, and an exotic blend of grenache, syrah and mourvèdre from Bonny Doon, I stayed with pinot noirs where I could find them. There weren't that many, ten in all in a show that showed 145 wineries, but there were a few outstanding wines, among them Ken Brown's Byron pinot noir from Santa Barbara county (owned by the Mondavis but with Brown as winemaker); and Robert Stemmler's fine offering from Sonoma, one of the few wineries other than Calera to use native or natural yeasts for fermenting pinot noir. There were also a few that seemed to me thin and insipid, and I wondered why they had been brought to the show – did bottle shock take them by surprise? I went so far as to venture a tactfully phrased question to a young man at one of the offending wineries, but he just snarled, and I moved off.

The heartbreak grape, clearly, was still breaking a few hearts, though it surprised me it was doing so quite so publicly.

Once the wines leave the winery or the San José warehouse (once, that is, the excise folk have taken their cut), they seem to exist only in sealed trucks, bonded premises, or in computer memories. Where do they go?

I followed my bottle of Calera Jensen 1987 through a customer consignment invoice on Calera's computer to the shipper in San José. From there it was packed into a massive semi-trailer with the products of a dozen other wineries; this trailer then joined a convoy of trucks heading for the east coast, a bootleg hijacker's wet dream. It crossed the desert in one pass, its refrigeration unit going full blast, passed over the prairies in a day and a half, and entered New Jersey no more than four days after it left. A few minutes after ten on a winter's morning it arrived in Somerville, New Jersey, the massive premises of Mark Lauber's Lauber Imports, where it became the property of burly, efficient men with forklifts, one pallet among thousands in a vast warehouse. The Calera label was nowhere to be seen, only an anonymous warehouse docket number. If it weren't that Lauber specializes in wine, and is as much a wine lover as a wholesaler, it might as well have been sardines, or computer motherboards, or footstools, or dental equipment, or canned peas. But the number could also be found in the memory banks of Lauber's computer system, where it was clearly identified by its place and name of origin (Calera, Hollister, California) and by its eventual consignee, one Peter Morrell. I found that the bottle was destined to take one more journey, this time to mid-town Manhattan.

The Morrell and Co. store on Madison Avenue is where our original dinner table host had purchased our Jensen pinot noir for his dinner party.

Morrell and Co. is on the ground floor of a banal high rise between 54th and 55th. There's nothing banal about the interior, however. Peter Morrell, the big, bluff, outgoing chairman, wine buyer, bon vivant and chief bottlewasher, second generation owner of a family business, has managed to impose a kind of measured calm on the store, with its wooden bins and attentive staff; and a much more dishevelled kind of order in the basement, where the stockrooms are, and in the sub-basement, where his cluttered office is to be found. He also operates a warehouse on E. 33rd Street and another temperature- and humidity-controlled warehouse for customers who want to store their own collections in bonded and air-conditioned safety. The store is a comforting place, with wooden bins of wine on three walls. There was a collection of ports on display, a range of sweet *eisweins*, a series of unusual California chardonnays, an excellent selection of Burgundies, and a sprinkling of odd lots and specials, mostly French and California, but also Italian, Spanish, Aussie and other wines, including a few from South Africa, like Nederburg and Kanonkop. I looked to see if there were any from the old de Villiers estate called Landskroon outside Paarl, but there weren't.

There's another Morrell store at Rockefeller Center; there was briefly a bistro and wine bar too, but it only lasted a year.

I reached Morrell's office by winding down a very tight spiral staircase to the stockroom level, then another staircase to the sub-basement. His office is not the home of an anal-retentive person. Its dominant mode is clutter. There were piles of paper everywhere, boxes, crates, bags of bottles, some full and some half-empty, standing, lying, jumbling up his desk. On the floor, a bottle of Chassagne-Montrachet was standing upright on the carpet next to an anonymous wine from the Midi. Just outside the door was a cardboard box of odd lots, waiting to accumulate enough bottles to justify a tasting. These are samples dropped off every day by hopeful winemakers, wholesalers and agents – "missionarymen" for the wineries, in the old phrase. There was also a crate of Pauillac, and on the wall certificates of various honours, French and American, including one from le Grand Conseil, l'académie du vin. Behind Morrell's desk (where a computer was perched precariously on some sort of makeshift shelf) were tottering piles of papers, and looseleaf binders containing every imaginable wine publication, up to date and well thumbed.

Morrell has long been a fan of Calera's wines. "It's important to us," he told me in 1992. "We sell a lot of it. I've been following Josh for ten years, and every year at the vintage change we open a bottle of the current vintage and a bottle of the new one, and up to now we have had no cause to worry. There are no surprises. There's just the familiar derivative, consistent quality. I always seem to prefer last year's to the current one, which I think is a good sign." He likes Calera because it is fairly priced, and has the complexity of style that he personally likes. "We sell out quickly. In retrospect, I should have held back six bottles of each Calera so we could keep some." That year Morrell sold 346 cases of Calera wines. "Not bad for one store, eh?"

Of the Jensen, only a case or two were ordered. Only two bottles were left when I was there.

I pointed to the wine periodicals, and asked him how he made his selections from the vast inventory of wines available to him.

"You can't possibly taste all the wines there are," I said.

"Yes we do," he said, misunderstanding. "At least 90 per cent of the stock we taste personally. "

"No," I said, "I mean, of all the wines in the world, how do you choose what to stock?"

Retailers, he said, find their wines through personal contacts, history, gossip, tours of the wine-producing regions, by dinners and formal tastings, and by attending wine shows. Bottles come from salespeople and anyone who drops by with a suggestion. Other ideas come from a voracious reading of the wine press. A good review will prompt an order, or at least a request for a sample, almost immediately, which is why the critics have such power in the industry. "These are generally experienced people and we learn to trust certain of them. They are reliable guiding lights. They miss a few, but not many." He also visits as many wineries as he can. "There's no substitute for experience; I want to check the dedication and techniques of the winemaker, to see if he is serious about what he does. Was the wine I tasted a fluke? Will he last? Wine after all is 50 per cent nature and 50 per cent man. That human 50 per cent can make all the difference between great wine and mediocre wine."

While we were talking there was a steady stream of calls. The Tastevin Society wanted to borrow a couple of barrels for their annual dinner, as they do every year; a caller wanted him to represent Georgian wines from Russia and Ukraine (he declined, averring that he is not an importer); people wanting to buy, to sell or just to invite him to dinner, lunch, a drink . . . Colleagues called, and customers.

Between calls, he punched up Calera on his computer, using a sophisticated inventory control software that he devised himself. It allows him to search for and tabulate by customer, by winery, by wine, by order, by quantity or by date. He hit a few buttons and a list of Calera's customers started to scroll up the screen. It was a formidable list, taking several minutes to roll by. I noticed a few who had ordered Calera by the case lot. There were individual collectors who bought in $1,000 lots.

He punched up the smaller number of clients who had bought the Calera single-vineyard wines. The Sellecks scrolled by, and the Reeds. There were the Jensens, the 1990s, the 1989s, the '88s, the '87s . . . I saw a familiar name, and an address in Mount Vernon.

I had found the bottle that started it all.

At the end of the evening, as the dishes were being done and the kitchen tidied, our host soaked the label off the bottle as an *aide mémoire* – he has a folder full of labels, each representing a pleasant memory. I looked at this folder some months later, and found the Jensen label in a plastic sleeve, between an Inniskillen icewine from the Niagara peninsula and an estate riesling from the south island of New Zealand. A few weeks after our visit, I noticed, our host had bought another Calera wine, the Central Coast pinot noir, and then a chardonnay. Well, in one way they were just more bytes for the Calera data-bank, more dollars for the bottom line. But I knew Jensen would be pleased far beyond these mundane matters. Never mind that he has mutated from visionary, from experimenter, from cutting edge, to Grand Old Man, to the Gold Standard, or that his winery has already passed its 30th birthday. None of that matters, in the end. "This year has rolled along very much like the previous 29," he wrote in one of his newsletters in 2006. "We've been busy growing grapes, making and selling wines, filling out forms for god knows how many government agencies, paying 'fees' (bribes), taxes and 'assessments' (more taxes), borrowing money from our dear bank, trying to pay the bank back, hiring and firing at will, cutting prices if absolutely necessary, raising them if at all possible, sucking up to all manner of people and companies with whom we do business, lording it over others who want our business, and generally causing havoc to the best of our abilities. Such is the modern way of business as practiced at Calera Wine Co." But it's more than this. By selling to our host in Mount Vernon, by happenstance or shrewd marketing, he had captured another wine lover, yes. But because of his obsession with quality and with consistency he had also become a page in a rich library of memories of a family he didn't know, while our host had in turn become part of the web of contacts that began in the gritty limestone soil of the Gavilan Mountains of central California. Not bad for the heartbreak grape.